Michael Smith's Complete Recipe Collection from Pebble Mill At One

Michael Smith is a specialist in English cookery and his books include *The Duchess of Duke Street Entertains, Fine English Cookery* and *Cookery with Michael Smith*. He began working on the Pebble Mill television programmes in 1976 and has been a regular and popular contributor to them ever since. In 1981/82 he won two Glenfiddich Awards – Writer of the Year and Book Author of the Year (Food). His recipes can also be tasted first-hand at three London restaurants, Waltons, The English House and the English Garden.

D1147243

MICHAEL SMITH'S COMPLETE RECIPE COLLECTION
FROM
PEBBLE MILL AT ONE

ARIEL BOOKS
BRITISH BROADCASTING CORPORATION

This collection first published 1982

Published by the British Broadcasting Corporation
35 Marylebone High Street, London WIM 4AA

Typeset by Phoenix Photosetting, Chatham
Printed in England by Mackays of Chatham

Set in 10/11pt Linotron Ehrhardt

ISBN 0 563 20093 6

Contents

Conversion tables

All these are approximate conversions which have either been rounded up or down. Never mix imperial and metric measures in one recipe, stick to one system or the other.

Oven temperature

Mark 1	275 F	140 C
2	300	150
3	325	170
4	350	180
5	375	190
6	400	200
7	425	220
8	450	230
9	475	240

Volume

2 fl oz	55ml
3	75
5 (¼ pt)	150
½ pt	275
¾	425
1	570
1¾	1 litre

Measurements

⅛ inch	3 mm
¼	5 mm
½	1
¾	2
1	2.5
1¼	3
1½	4
1¾	4.5
2	5
3	7.5
4	10
5	13
6	15
7	18
8	20
9	23
10	25.5
11	28
12	30

Weights

½ oz	10 g
1	25
1½	40
2	50
2½	60
3	75
4	110
4½	125
5	150
6	175
7	200
8	225
9	250
10	275
12	350
1 lb	450
1½	700
2	900
3	1 kg 350 g

Introduction

1976 was a very special year for me. Not only did I go to New York to supervise the Bicentennial Dinner of the International Wine and Food Society, I was, for almost eighteen months, heavily involved in the technical and academic research and actual manifestation of all the magnificent food scenes the public enjoyed so much in the BBC's epic series *The Duchess of Duke Street*. It was also the first year that I began my cookery programmes for Pebble Mill.

The great interest in the *Duchess* was a natural follow-on from the fictional *Upstairs, Downstairs* and many of the other major historical series for which British television holds a worldwide reputation for excellence.

I have been chauvinist all my life about English cookery and I have used it as a basis for my food writings (as well as actual cooking). I believe that a country needs, and should have, a national bill-of-fare or kitchen, (I find the word *cuisine* sticks in my pen nib!).

The luxury of being able to restore, through the small screen, much of what has been lost in the history of our kitchens – not so much in our own homes – but in our restaurants and hotels, was a golden opportunity and not to be missed.

I had found it strange, when I first returned to this country after my training abroad in the hotel schools and restaurants of Switzerland and France (for there was but one 'catering' school in England back in 1947) that the only decent food available to the British public was that from other countries like France and Italy, Spain and Portugal, China, Thailand and, more recently, the fast foods of the United States.

And yet in the pages of our history books there is ample evidence of fine things of a truly English nature. One has only to look through the writings of Jane Austen, Shakespeare, Sydney Smith, the diaries of John Evelyn and Parson Woodford to find ample evidence of a national diet.

The recipes, or receipts as they were called for centuries, are however, meticulously recorded in the numerous books on cookery and household management which were abundant in the seventeenth, eighteenth and nineteenth centuries, and in manuscripts before that time. Just why and when and how all this good food disappeared is veiled, if not in mystery, then in a fog of social and religious history, and is a story too complex to relate here even if I had a secure enough knowledge to tell it.

Pebble Mill at One helped me show the strengths of English cookery through the small screen. I was asked to do a short series of eight cookery demonstrations using those recipes which I considered the most important from our antique cookery books, and which I felt ought to be restored to our repertory.

Grace and Flavour was born in the autumn of 1976. It proved so popular with the viewing public that *More Grace and Flavour* followed in 1977 – the book sales for these first two series sold over a *quarter of a million* copies! Evidence enough that there was abundant interest in English recipes. That the powers-that-be cannot yet be persuaded to extend such a series is an obvious disappointment to me, but one which I continue to hope will soon be rectified, and in some small way this has started to happen in *Negus Enjoys*.

Having established a happy rapport with lunchtime viewers whose numbers often top five million, there followed other series on different themes, even 'going abroad' as with *Grace and Flavour à la Mode*. The re-establishing of some of the basics of all cookery in *The Saucy Cookbook* proved popular with the more serious cook and encouraged my producer to let me move into a specialised field with *A Fine Kettle of Fish*. This was to encourage a people living on an island surrounded by fish-filled waters – yet with few interesting dishes to show for it.

The Sandwich Book took a look at the interesting ideas other countries offered for this 'snack'. The *Croque Monsieur* of France, Italy's *Mozzarella in Carroza*, the hundred of varieties of open sandwiches from Denmark, and the Hamburger and Club sandwich of America. All of these make useful light meals in our hectic daily lives, our own afternoon tea sandwiches being too delicate to satisfy hunger pangs.

More recently, I have enjoyed working in a field I like immensely. *Just Desserts* – hitting Number Three in the *Sunday Times* paperback bestseller list – is proof enough that the British housewife has not deserted that area in her kitchen where she perhaps excels the most. It is also vindication for me that we still do set great store by the effort required in the making of breads, cakes, puddings and other sweets. It is in this area of cookery that Britain has more to offer than any other country in the world, and it's an area where the British housewife is still expanding.

It is perhaps disappointing that in the main courses of our repertory this development is not so evident. Hopefully my *Complete Recipe Collection from Pebble Mill at One* will help rectify this shortfall somewhat, as you are tempted to try poached plaice with oranges and anchovy on p. 80 or the exotic pork with fruits and spices, Elizabethan pork, on p. 55.

Here then, for those who like to keep their bookshelves tidy and in order, and for those viewers who perhaps missed out on one or other of the booklets, and – even more importantly for those who are not lucky enough to be free to watch *Pebble Mill at One* at lunchtime – I have brought all the Pebble Mill booklets together into one volume.

Some twenty new recipes have been added, bringing the total number of recipes to 270. These new recipes have a modern slant. I'm sure you will enjoy making and *eating* such things as Chilled cream of tomato soup with turmeric and orange for a special summer dinner party. Minced beef cobbler pie for family Sunday lunch, as a joint can be so costly these days: and do try Wensleydale soufflé tarts which slot into almost any meal from the main event at high tea to an elegant starter at dinner time.

A tangy lemon pudding for afters on a cold day or a rich Sabayon au Rhum as a finish to an elegant supper are all within the bounds of possibility for you.

It now only remains for me to say thank you to those who have watched the programme over the past six years and welcome to new readers – I hope you will be converted to my philosophy on English (and other) food.

Enjoy the time you spend in your kitchen, which is where I feel I can most help you, and – for this is what it's all about – enjoy the partaking.

Michael Smith
London, May 1982

Soups

Tomato and chive soup 12
Chilled cream tomato soup with turmeric, orange
and shrimps 12
Cauliflower soup 13
Beetroot and orange soup 14
Soupè a l'Oignon (Parisienne onion soup) 15
Sweetcorn chowder 15
Chilled fennel soup 16
Green lentil and Italian sausage soup 17
Aigo-Saou (Fish and garlic soup) 18
Cornish crab soup 19
Royal turtle soup with Queen Mary's cheese biscuits 20
Rich game soup 20

Tomato and chive soup

Serves 4

The tomato came into popular use rather late in the eighteenth century, but has since forged a firm place in English cooking, particularly in the form of soup.

6 oz tomato purée	2 oz flour
1 large onion	1½ pints stock
1 large carrot	(use stock cube)
1 leek	½ pint tinned tomato juice
2 cloves garlic crushed	1 glass medium dry white wine
tip of a tsp curry powder	(optional)
2 oz butter	Salt, freshly milled pepper

Garnish
2 tomatoes
2 tbsp chopped chives

¼ pint double cream

Clean, peel and slice vegetables. Skin, deseed and chop the tomato for the garnish. Finely snip the chives with a pair of scissors.

Melt butter in heavy-bottomed pan without letting it colour. Add onion, garlic, carrot, leek, and the modicum of curry powder. Fry them gently for a few minutes without permitting them to acquire too much colour and stirring them around from time to time.

Add the purée, stir in the flour and immediately reduce the heat (tomato purée easily burns). Add the white wine, stock, seasoning and tomato juice, stir all together and simmer over a low heat for one hour.

Strain the soup, half whip the cream, swirl this into the finished soup to give a somewhat marbled effect; add chives and the chopped tomato to each individual serving.

Chilled cream tomato soup with turmeric, orange and shrimps

Serves 4 or 5

Whilst I think this soup is at its best when served well chilled and in smallish portions as it is very rich, it can be served hot.

14 fl oz tomato juice
1 level tsp turmeric
1 level tsp mild curry powder
1 clove garlic, crushed
½ pint double cream

1 tsp castor sugar
Juice of half a lemon
1 heaped tsp of finely grated
   rind of orange

Garnish
2 navel oranges, segmented
2 tomatoes, skinned, deseeded
   and cut into dice

4 oz peeled shrimps
   (frozen or fresh)

Put all the ingredients except the cream into a heavy-bottomed pan, bring to the boil and simmer for 10 minutes.

Add the cream and simmer for a further 10 minutes.

Leave to cool. Strain into a bowl, cover with cling-film and chill well, preferably overnight.

Ladle into chilled soup cups, and garnish with a little of the diced tomato, two or three orange segments and the shrimps.

Cauliflower soup

Serves 5 or 6

2 pints chicken stock
1 small tight flowered
   cauliflower
¼ pint double cream
1 tsp lime mustard (or other
   mild French mustard)

¼ tsp nutmeg
1 poached egg per serving
Beurre-manié (2 oz softened
   butter, 1 oz flour made into
   a soft paste)
Salt and pepper

To poach the eggs
Poach the eggs in advance and store in a dish of cold water. (The heat of the soup will be sufficient to warm them through in the individual bowls). Select a shallow pan or frying pan. Lightly oil the bottom. Pour in an inch of water, put in a half-teaspoon of salt.

As soon as the water is simmering, but not boiling, break eggs into a cup, one at a time. Make a whirlpool in the water with a teaspoon, slide the egg into this and collect the white around the yolk with a slotted spoon. Leave to poach until cooked. Lift out carefully with a slotted spoon, and lower gently into the dish of cold water. When cold, trim off any straggling bits of egg white: this is just to neaten things off.

To make the soup

Break the cauliflower into tiny florets. Bring the stock to the boil with the cauliflower stalk cut into pieces. Strain these out.

Put in the cauliflower pieces and simmer until just cooked: they should still be crisp. Remove to a dish with a slotted spoon, or strain into a second pan.

Add the cream and bring to the boil. Whisk in the mustard and sprinkle in the nutmeg: bring to the boil again and test for salt and pepper.

Whisk in little bits of the *beurre-manié*, allowing the soup to return to the boil between each addition. The finished soup should be the consistency of single cream. Lower the heat and simmer for five minutes.

Return the cauliflower florets to the pan to heat them through. Place a poached egg in the bottom of each soup bowl, and carefully ladle over the steaming soup.

Note: Any remaining *beurre-manié* can be stored in a plastic-lidded container in the fridge for future use, but you will probably need it all.

Beetroot and orange soup

Serves 4

¾ lb boiled beetroots
6 spring onions
¾ pint cold stock (from chicken stock cube)
1 tsp orange rind
¼ pint orange juice

½ tsp ground mace
A little salt
1 tbsp tarragon or red wine vinegar
1 tbsp good olive oil

Garnish (optional)
Snipped chives or parsley

Orange segments

Grate the beetroots on the coarse side of a grater. Finely shred the spring onions. Mix all the ingredients except the oil together, retaining ¼ pint of the stock so that you can adjust the consistency of the soup to your liking. Chill very well.

Just before serving, stir in the all-essential olive oil to give the soup sparkle and brightness. Serve in chilled soup cups garnished with orange segments. Sprinkle with the chives or parsley.

Soupe à l'Oignon (Parisienne onion soup)

Serves 4

This is the recipe I learned to use when I was working in Paris back in the fifties.

8 oz onions
2 oz butter
½ oz flour
1 pint water
Salt
Freshly milled black pepper

Garnish
French bread
1–2 oz Gruyère or other
   melting cheese
1 oz butter

Slice the onions as thinly as possible. Fry them gently in the butter until an even and deep golden brown. Sprinkle over the flour and stir well and continue to cook for 2 to 3 minutes. Gradually stir in the water. Season lightly and simmer for 15 minutes.

Cut dry, but not stale, French bread (the one they call '*flûte*') into discs ¼ inch thick. Fry these gently in a further ounce or so of butter until crisp. Sprinkle with grated cheese.

Fill ovenproof soup bowls with the onion soup. Float two or three cheese croûtons on top and brown in a hot oven or medium hot grill until the cheese is melted golden brown and bubbling.

Sweetcorn chowder

Serves 6, with some left over for seconds!

Chowder gets its name from the old French word for a provincial cooking pot . . . a *chaudière*.

Very popular in America and growing in popularity over here, a chowder is often made with clams, oysters or other shell fish: Corn Chowder is a cheaper but not-to-be-scorned type of dish. Filling and warming on a winter's day or a stormy night.

12 oz tin sweetcorn, drained
   and rinsed under cold water
2 onions, finely chopped
Half-a-head celery, cleaned
   and chopped into small dice
4 rashers bacon,
   cut into small dice

4 large waxy potatoes, peeled
   and cut into small dice *see*
   Method
3 pints chicken stock
3 oz butter

Special seasonings
4 dashes Tabasco sauce
1 tbsp Worcester sauce

Juice of half a lemon

To 'finish' the chowder
½ pint single cream

3 egg yolks

To garnish the chowder (optional)
8 oz piece salt pork
Butter

4 slices of white bread

Cut the potato into ¼ inch dice if you can manage to get the dice that small. Cook the potatoes in some of the chicken stock until just tender. Strain retaining the liquid.

Melt the butter in a large heavy-bottomed pan, and fry the bacon in this until crisp.

Remove the bacon with a draining spoon, and put to one side whilst you fry the onion and celery over a low heat until transparent and tender.

Add the sweetcorn and the stock and potato liquid. Bring to the boil and simmer for half an hour. Add the special seasonings, and return the potatoes to the pan to get hot right through.

Just before serving, line up your warm soup bowls on a tray. Whisk the egg yolks with the cream and pour directly into the boiling hot chowder, stirring well as you do so.

Ladle into the bowls and top with the garnish, which whilst I say it is optional, is a very desirable addition!

To make the garnish
Cut slices of bread into half inch cubes, and fry these in butter until they are crisp and golden brown. Do this slowly so that they brown evenly and don't burn. Cut the salt pork into ¼ inch dice and fry this slowly and patiently until crisp right through, an essential factor.

Chilled fennel soup

Serves 4

2 heads fennel (about 3 lbs)
Chicken stock or stock cube
   see Method
1 pint double cream

1 tsp fennel seeds tied in
   muslin
Salt and milled white pepper

Clean and quarter the fennel (reserve the fronds in cold water).

Cover with chicken stock, add the seeds, and simmer until tender. Season carefully.

Blend to a fine but thick purée using a little of the cooking stock. (Cool and reserve the rest.)

For a really fine soup, laboriously press the purée through a hair sieve after blending.

Add enough cream to give a delicate consistency. Chill well.

Before serving, thin down the soup with some of the chilled reserved stock if necessary.

Garnish with a little of the chopped fennel fronds.

If freezing the soup for storing, add the chopped fennel fronds when the soup is cold, but before freezing.

Green lentil and Italian sausage soup
Serves 4

I have devised this wholesome soup to retain the full texture of the lentils which, whilst called green, are in fact more of a muddy grey colour. Any lentils, red or yellow, can be substituted.

8 oz green lentils soaked overnight in boiling water to cover
2 onions, chopped
4 large sticks celery, chopped
1 clove garlic, crushed
1½ pints chicken stock
1 bay leaf   ⎱ or 1 bouquet
1 sprig thyme ⎰ garni sachet

6 oz piece Italian smoked sausage (or other Continental sausage of your liking)
4 oz piece of boiling bacon or hock
Salt and pepper if necessary. This will depend on the saltiness of the sausages and bacon

Using ½ pint of the stock, in a blender or food processor, make a purée of the onions, celery and garlic.

Drain the lentils and rinse them well under cold running water. Put them with the purée, herbs or bouquet garni, sausage and bacon, and the remaining stock into a heavy bottomed pan: bring to the boil and simmer until the lentils are tender but not a total mush. Season if necessary.

Skim off any scum which rises to the surface early in the cooking process.

Remove the sausage, bacon and herbs, or bouquet garni which

should be discarded. Cut the sausage into discs or pieces, and shred the bacon into manageable bits. Put a little of each into a soup bowl and ladle over the boiling soup.

Aigo-Saou (Fish and garlic soup)

Serves 4 as a main course soup

3 lb white fish (haddock, cod, whiting)	Bouquet of herbs (sprig thyme, 1 bay leaf, large sprig parsley tied between two pieces celery)
8 oz sliced onion	
2 large tomatoes, skinned, deseeded and chopped	
4 medium potatoes, peeled, cut into inch cubes	4 tbsp olive oil
	Salt and pepper
	Fish stock or water
4 cloves garlic, crushed	Parmesan or Cheddar cheese

Cut the fish into 2 inch pieces. Place all the ingredients except the cheese into a large pan (not aluminium as this tends to discolour). Douse with the olive oil. Pour over enough fish stock or cold water to just cover. Bring to the boil and allow to bubble for 15 minutes, or until the potatoes are tender.

Serve the bouillon (liquid) as a soup with croûtons and freshly grated Parmesan or mature Cheddar cheese.

Serve the fish and potatoes as a main course with garlic or green mayonnaise.

For those who like *rouille* – a red pepper relish – a small spoon of this can be added to each serving. (Pound 4 cloves crushed garlic, 2 red peppers, skinned and seeded, 1 oz soft white bread crumbs, 4 tbsp olive oil and a pinch of cayenne in a mortar or blend in a machine until you have a smooth paste.)

Cornish crab soup

Serves 4

½ lb crab meat (half dark, half white), defrosted if frozen	1 oz white flour
	Grated rind of 1 orange
1 large onion	½ pint double cream
1 clove garlic	1 glass dry sherry
2 pints fish stock (or chicken stock)	Salt and freshly ground white pepper
2 oz butter	

Slice the onion and crush the garlic. Melt the butter in a heavy-bottomed pan. When just foaming, but not coloured, add the onion and garlic. Cover with a lid and soften the onion without colouring.

Add the de-frosted dark crab meat and work in well. Add the flour, stirring in well to avoid lumping. Slowly add the stock, stirring all the time until the soup boils. Simmer for 30 minutes. Strain the soup into a clean pan. Season with salt and pepper; add the cream, sherry and orange rind.

Chop the de-frosted white crab meat and remove any 'blades'. Add the fish to the soup, re-heat and serve immediately.

Royal turtle soup

Turtle soup is bought in tins these days – I suggest you do likewise, or employ a cheaper version by using a good brand of tinned consommé to which add a good glass of sherry or Madeira. Serve with the following cheese biscuits, said by Queen Mary's chef, Gabriel Tschumi, to have been very popular with her.

Queen Mary's cheese biscuits

4 oz plain flour	1 egg yolk
3 oz good butter	A little salt
2 oz grated fresh Parmesan cheese	Tip of a tsp nutmeg

Rub butter into flour. Dredge in grated cheese and seasonings, bind with egg yolk. Do not add any additional water. Leave to rest. Roll out thinly (¼ inch thick) cut into 1½ inch circles (the pastry is too fragile for larger biscuits). Bake at gas mark 5, 375°F (190°C), for 7–10 minutes.

These biscuits will melt in your mouth.

Rich game soup
Serves 8 to 10

A good game soup cannot be made without good ingredients (nor can anything for that matter), so assuming that you have decided to make the soup, the quantity I give is for upwards of eight servings. It is rich and gamey, and worth every ounce of effort you put into it.

½ a hare, fresh or frozen	4 pints game stock made from the bones
1 old grouse or pheasant, fresh or frozen	3 tbsp tomato purée
8 oz lean ham	1 pint red wine
8 oz stewing steak, weighed *without fat*	8 cloves
2 oz butter	3 bay leaves
3 oz flour	1 tsp thyme
4 tbsp olive oil	4 fl. oz glass tawny port
2 large carrots	Salt and freshly ground pepper
1 large onion	Gravy browning (natural colouring) (optional)
8 oz field mushrooms	Knob of butter
2 stalks celery	

Garnish
The breasts and liver of the
grouse or pheasant

Clean, peel and cube the carrots, onion and celery. Slice the mushrooms.

Strip the raw meat off the hare and the grouse or pheasant. Cover the bones with cold water (about 4 pints), bring to the boil, skim well and simmer for 2 hours, adding an extra ½ pint of water after the first hour. Do not season. Strain, and reserve stock.

Cut all the meat, except the grouse or pheasant breasts and liver into cubes. Take a large plastic bag, put in the flour, salt and pepper and shake the cubes of meat in this until they are thoroughly coated.

Melt the butter and oil together in a large pan. Add the vegetables (except the mushrooms) gradually and fry them over a good heat, taking care to brown them without burning. Stir them constantly.

Remove the browned vegetables to a platter and in the remaining fat brown all the meat cubes. Add the uncut breasts and vegetables to the pan and shake over them any remaining flour.

Add the tomato purée and the mushrooms. Lower the heat and, stirring all the while, let all this acquire a good brown colour. Pour over 3 pints of strained stock and the red wine. Add all the seasonings. The breasts of the grouse or pheasant will be cooked in 15 minutes. Remove these and allow them to cool before cutting them into ¼ inch dice. Set aside for the garnish.

Cook the rest of the soup very slowly for 2½ to 3 hours, occasionally stirring well to ensure that nothing is sticking to the bottom.

Strain the soup and check the seasoning. Bring the quantity up to 4 or 5 pints, depending how thick you like it, using the remaining stock. Skim off any fat that has risen to the surface.

If great care has been taken with the frying at all the different stages, the soup should be rich, brown and glossy. If not, add a little brown colouring (not gravy powder), for the soup must look bold and strong, and adjusting colour is as important as adjusting thickening and seasoning.

Quickly fry the liver in a knob of butter and cut into dice. Reheat the soup, and just before serving add the diced breasts and liver and the port.

Hot starters

Cheese 'pye' 23
Asparagus tarts 24
Quiche Lorraine (Egg and bacon flan) 24
Pilchard quiche 25
Wensleydale soufflé tarts with smoked fish 26
Eggs in cases 27
Stuffed tomatoes 27
Stuffed pancakes 28
Bacon and Asparagus 'Fraze' 29
'Fricassey' of eggs 29
Avocado Pebble Mill 30
Mariner style mussels (Moules marinières) 31
Brandade de morue
(Hot purée of salt cod with garlic and cream) 32

Cheese 'pye'

Serves 5 or 6

It doesn't take a professional to recognise England's answer to the now-popular quiche. However, do try this pie as a chauvinistic dish to set before your guests using, of course, its ethnic name! At one time a flan case was called a coffin! But it was always made with 'good sweet butter'.

Pastry
8 oz plain flour
5 oz unsalted butter

1 egg yolk beaten with ½ cup
  iced water

Filling
¾ pint single cream
6 eggs
4 oz grated dry cheese (mild
  Cheddar)

Salt and freshly milled white
  pepper or nutmeg

Rub the butter into the flour until the mixture is sandy textured. (I don't use salt in my pastry; others do, so add a pinch to the flour if you prefer.) Make a well and add the beaten egg and water at one fell swoop; quickly gather into a light dough and leave to rest in a cool place for half an hour. Roll out and line a 1½ inch deep flan ring or pie plate. Line with foil – or paper and dried peas – bake 'blind' at gas mark 6, 400°F (200°C) until almost cooked.

Now beat the eggs, season lightly with salt and pepper or nutmeg. Bring the cream to the boil, pour on to the beaten eggs stirring until all is combined.

Evenly cover the flan case with the grated cheese, reserving a third of it for the top. Strain in the egg mixture and return the flan to the oven, this time at gas mark 3, 325°F (170°C) for 30 minutes or until the custard is set. After 15 minutes of the baking time sprinkle the remaining cheese on top.

Whilst this pie was probably originally served cold, I think it is better for being eaten hot or at least warm. If you want to make it in advance, leave the filling slightly undercooked so that when it is warmed up it is still light.

Asparagus tarts

Serves 6

8 oz frozen asparagus tips
¼ pint single cream
¼ pint milk
3 eggs

½ tsp grated nutmeg
½ oz good unsalted butter
Salt
8 oz shortcrust pastry
(frozen is excellent)

Line 3 inch diameter tartlet tins with thinly rolled pastry to make six tarts. Line pastry with lightly buttered foil and bake 'blind' at gas mark 6, 400°F (200°C) for 15 minutes. Remove lining.

Beat eggs with seasonings. Bring cream and milk to boil, pour over and whisk in. Cut off tips of asparagus and simmer gently in lightly salted water for 5 minutes. Drain and put on one side. Simmer remainder of asparagus until tender. Drain and put through blender together with cream mixture. Strain through a hair-sieve to remove 'strings' which a blender often cannot cope with.

Fill tartlets with mixture, add three or four spears to each and bake at gas mark 3, 275°F (140°C) for a further 25 minutes or until just set. Spread a little good unsalted butter over the surface of each tart just before serving hot.

If the tarts are cooked in advance, leave the cream filling slightly undercooked and reheat at gas mark 3, 275°F (140°C).

Quiche Lorraine (Egg and bacon flan)

Serves 5 or 6

Just what has happened to the quiche since its arrival in Britain after the war shows all too sadly what often happens to food in this country if we don't occasionally 'revenir à nos moutons' or go back to square one.

Theories vary, even in Alsace/Lorraine, regarding the ingredients of the quiche but some factors are unchanging. It is made of pastry, eggs and cream and is enriched with bacon, and perhaps Swiss cheese and onion.

Here then is my recipe, used now for nigh on 30 years and learned at the stove of my mother-in-law who was brought up in France.

Pastry

Use the recipe on page 23 omitting the sugar and adding two pinches of salt.

Bake a pastry shell totally blind, ideally using an 8 × 1½ inch deep flan ring.

Filling

¾ pint single cream
5 eggs
½ oz butter
1 small onion finely chopped
2 oz good bacon, cut into
   striplets

1 oz freshly grated Gruyère or
   Parmesan cheese
Nutmeg
An extra 2 oz unsalted butter
Salt and pepper

Lightly fry the bacon and onion in a modicum of butter until a pale golden colour.

Scatter the bacon and onion over the base of the baked pastry shell (leave the metal ring in place). Beat the eggs with a little salt and pepper.

Bring the cream to the boil and pour over the eggs whilst beating.

Strain the mixture carefully into the pastry shell, grate over a little nutmeg and put to bake at gas mark 3, 325°F (170°C).

After 20 minutes, when a skin has formed, scatter the cheese over and return the quiche to the oven until lightly browned and just set (this will take another 20 minutes or even longer).

Just before serving – and a quiche must be served piping hot – spread the unsalted butter over the entire surface. You will now have a feather-light savoury custard in a buttery-crisp pastry case glistening with honest French butter.

Pilchard quiche

Serves 5 or 6

6 oz shortcrust pastry

Filling

2 eggs
4 oz grated cheese
1 bunch spring onions or
   1 medium sized onion
2 yolks

¼ pint milk
1 oz butter
1 × 8 oz can pilchards,
   skinned, boned and mashed
Salt and milled pepper

Line an 8 inch flan ring with the pastry. Bake biind.

Prepare the filling by beating the eggs and yolks in a basin, adding the cheese, seasoning and milk. Melt the butter in a saucepan and brown the finely sliced onions. Cook slowly till just golden-brown and then add to the mixture.

Add the pilchards and pour into the pastry case. Bake at gas mark 5, 375°F (190°C) until firm and golden-brown – approximately 30 minutes. Serve hot or cold.

Wensleydale soufflé tarts with smoked fish

Serves 6

12 oz shortcrust pastry to line
6 × 3 inch loose bottomed tart
  tins
8 oz minced or chopped

smoked fish such as salmon, trout, haddock mixed with 1 tsp mild French mustard

For the soufflé mixture
1 oz plain white flour
1½ oz butter
Scant ½ pint cold milk
4 oz Wensleydale cheese,
  grated

4 egg yolks, beaten
5 egg whites
Salt, milled white pepper, or
  nutmeg

Bake the pastry shells blind (the day before if you like). Return them to their tins and spread the fish mixture equally between the six.

In advance make up the basic sauce. Melt the butter, stir in the flour, gradually add the cold milk stirring briskly until you have a smooth white sauce. Add the grated cheese and cook the sauce for 2 to 3 minutes. Season well (remembering to allow for the bulk of beaten egg whites). Remove the pan from the heat and add the beaten yolks. Leave to cool, covered with a circle of buttered paper to prevent a skin from forming. Whisk the egg whites until they *just* stand in peaks. Mix one-third of these into the sauce thoroughly. Fold and 'cut' in the remainder using a slotted spoon for this operation. Pour the mixture into the tarts, filling them. Bake in a pre-heated oven gas mark 7, 425°F (220°C), for 15 minutes or until risen, golden brown and set.

Eggs in cases

Serves 6

8 oz shortcrust pastry (frozen
  is excellent)
4 oz minced boiled ham
1 heaped tbsp chopped chives
  (or parsley)

12 eggs
6 tbsp single cream
Salt and freshly milled pepper

Line 3 inch diameter tart tins with pastry to make six tarts. Line pastry with lightly buttered foil and bake blind at gas mark 6, 400°F (200°C) for 15 minutes. Remove lining.

Mix ham with chives or parsley and bind with a modicum of cream. Season lightly. Divide between the six cases, spreading evenly over the bottom.

Break two eggs into each case. Season lightly and pour a tablespoon of cream over the top.

Bake at gas mark 4, 350°F (180°C) until eggs are set.

Stuffed tomatoes

Serves 8

2 large sticks celery
1 medium onion
4 oz rice
2 fl. oz water
1 lb smoked haddock
1 bay leaf
8 peppercorns

1 tsp freshly chopped thyme
  (or ½ tsp dried)
Salt and pepper
8 large firm tomatoes
1 tbsp tomato pureé
2 oz softened butter

Finely chop celery and onion, and together with rice turn into the water when it boils. Simmer for about 30 minutes until rice is cooked. Drain thoroughly.

Meanwhile poach haddock with bay leaf and peppercorns in a little water or milk (about 10 minutes) until cooked. Remove haddock from cooking liquor, skin, bone and flake. Mix with cooked rice mixture, thyme, salt and pepper.

Remove a slice from the top of each tomato. Scoop out seeds and discard. Add a good knob of softened butter to the fish mixture. Pack the tomatoes with this filling, piling generously, then placing each slice back on top. Add tomato pureé to remaining filling and put this mixture into an ovenproof dish. Stand the tomatoes on top making a small hollow for each. Bake in oven gas mark 6, 400°F (200°C), for 20 minutes.

A really colourful dish as a starter for eight people. Serve with a watercress salad and buttered brown toast.

Stuffed pancakes
Serves 8

Pancake batter

3 oz wholemeal flour	2 eggs
3 oz plain white flour	½ pint milk
1 tsp salt	

Stuffing

1 small onion, finely chopped	12 oz smoked mackerel
2 tbsp chopped parsley	3 tbsp lemon juice
1 tbsp butter or nut oil	Salt and pepper
1 oz butter	8 oz frozen chopped spinach
Oil for frying	Lemon wedges

Sift the flours and salt together into a bowl, add eggs and a quarter of the milk. Beat together, then gradually beat in remaining milk and a little water if necessary. Cover and set aside.

To make the filling, sauté onion and parsley in the butter until onion softens. Skin, bone and flake the mackerel and add to the onion with lemon juice, salt and pepper. Heat gently for 10 minutes and keep warm.

Cook spinach as directed on packet. Drain well, and add butter. Keep warm.

Make at least 8 pancakes. Keep them hot on a plate over a pan of hot water, placing greaseproof paper between them and covering the pile with foil.

Put a generous tablespoonful of stuffing on a pancake and roll up. Repeat with 7 pancakes. Spoon spinach partially over fish-stuffed pancakes. Garnish with lemon wedges.

One stuffed pancake per person makes a useful starter to a meal, while two per person are quite filling. The addition of wholemeal flour makes pancakes more substantial and produces a delicious nutty flavour. Spinach contrasts well with the other flavours and textures thus making a sauce unnecessary.

Bacon and asparagus 'Fraze'

Serves 4

The 'Fraze' is an old English pancake-cum-omelet and could well find its way back into our bills of fare either for breakfast, lunch or supper.

Batter

2 eggs
1 oz flour
¼ pint single cream or milk

Water if necessary
Salt and pepper
Butter

Filling

Fried onions
Crisply fried bacon strips

Asparagus tips

Make up the batter in the usual way. Fry the pancakes in butter, adding the filling (you can use as much or as little as you like) just before turning to cook on the second side.

Serve as quickly as possible whilst the frazes are still hot and soft.

'Fricassey' of eggs

Serves 6

Fricassey was at one time a common method of preparing foods in a creamy sauce. This way of preparing eggs is different and economical for tea, supper, as a starter for dinner, or even for breakfast.

6 eggs
¼ pint milk
¼ pint single cream
Scant 1 oz flour
1½ oz butter
Tiny onion

1 tbsp freshly chopped chives
(or the palest green part of spring onions)
Salt and pepper or nutmeg
3 slices good white bread
Butter for frying

With a fancy cutter stamp out six rounds of bread 2 inches in diameter and about ¼ inch thick. Fry these in butter until golden brown and crisp.

Finely chop the onion. Melt the butter but don't allow it to take any colour. Soften the onion in this. Stir in the flour and gradually incorporate the milk and then the cream; beat until the sauce is smooth as velvet. Cook over a gentle heat for 2 to 3 minutes. Season with salt and pepper or a little grated nutmeg. Cover the surface of the sauce with a circle of buttered paper and stand the pan in a second pan of gently simmering water until ready for use.

Boil the eggs for no more than 8 minutes. Run them under cold water and shell them. The yolks should have just a modicum of softness in the centre and not be bullet-hard! Mash the yolks and beat into the waiting sauce. Cut the whites into striplets and fold in carefully together with the chives. Pile the fricassey onto the hot bread shapes and serve immediately.

Avocado Pebble Mill
Serves 4

This is probably one of the richest starters you will ever taste, so serve with a very modest and plain main course and an even more modest pudding.

2 ripe avocado pears
Lemon juice
½ pint chicken stock (from stock cube)

½ pint Sauce Béarnaise (page 125)
4 eggs
Freshly-milled black pepper

First make up the Sauce Béarnaise and keep warm.

Poach or lightly boil the eggs. Cut the avocado pears in half, remove the stone and rub the exposed surface with lemon juice.

Select a shallow pan just large enough to contain the pears face down. Bring the stock to the boil and pour over the pears in the pan. Heat through over minimum heat (approximately 5 minutes).

Arrange each pear in an individual dish. If you use boiled eggs (easier), shell them and pop an egg into each stone pit. Sprinkle over a little extra lemon juice for astringency and a little freshly-milled black pepper. Coat with Sauce Béarnaise and serve immediately with fingers of dry wholemeal toast. Eat the pears with a teaspoon.

Mariner-style mussels (Moules Marinières)
Serves 4

Some recipes call for cream, some don't. I use it, but it is optional.

4 dozen fresh mussels
1 medium onion (2 to 3 oz)
　very finely chopped
2 oz French or Dutch butter
¾ pint dry white wine (such as
　a Muscadet or Chablis)
1 sprig fresh thyme (or level
　teaspoon dried thyme)

1 small bay leaf
Squeeze lemon juice
Freshly milled white (or black)
　pepper
Salt
½ pint single cream

Thickening agent
2 oz butter and 1 oz flour
mashed with a fork into
a soft paste

Garnish
2 tbsp chopped parsley

To clean mussels
Wash under running cold water brushing away any dirt or loose barnacles with a stiff or wire brush. Discard cracked or open shells. Remove the 'beards'.

In a large heavy-bottomed pan, melt the butter and soften the chopped onion until transparent without letting it colour. Add the wine, herbs, a little pepper and a good squeeze of lemon juice. Simmer for 10 minutes to extract the flavours.

Put the mussels into the pan, cover with a lid and steam the mussels, shaking the pan gently all the while, until the shells open. Discard any that remain closed. With a draining spoon or skimmer, remove the mussels to a warm tureen or large bowl, removing and discarding the top shells of each mussel as you go along (a nicety but not essential). Cover with a wetted cloth, then a lid and keep warm in the oven at gas mark ½, 250°F (130°C). Now, reduce the cooking liquor to half its original quantity by boiling *rapidly* (this won't take more than 2 to 3 minutes).

Lower the heat, pour in the cream, check the seasoning. Whisk in little bits of the butter and flour paste (*beurre-manié*) allowing the 'sauce' or 'soup' to bubble between each little addition. Add ⅔ of the parsley. The finished liquor should be no thicker than single cream. Pour over the waiting mussels, sprinkle over the remaining parsley and serve immediately.

Brandade de morue
(Hot purée of salt cod with garlic and cream)

Serves 6

Patience and effort will bring the best results when making a *brandade* which is a cross between a pâté and a purée but is served hot on buttered toast. The salt cod must be soaked for 24 hours and the water should be changed at least 4 times during the soaking.

2 lb salt cod, soaked	Juice of half lemon
2 cloves garlic, crushed	¼ tsp pepper
5 fl oz olive oil, warmed	¼ tsp nutmeg
5 fl oz warm milk	2 tbsp double cream

Cover the cod, after soaking, with cold water, bring to the boil and simmer for 20 minutes. Drain, cool and remove all skin and bones. Put the flesh into a blender or food processor with the crushed garlic and 1 tablespoon of the warmed oil. Give it a turn or two.

Then gradually incorporate the warm oil and warmed (not hot) milk, alternately adding a spoonful at a time.

Transfer the mixture to a double boiler (or a pan which fits inside a larger pan) and heat, stirring frequently. Add the cream, lemon juice, nutmeg and seasoning. Obviously further salt should not be needed, but just in case you have soaked too much salt out, taste it.

The consistency should be that of well mashed and creamed potatoes. (If you don't possess a blender or similar machine then the cod must be first minced then laboriously pounded in a mortar or stainless steel bowl using the butt of a rolling pin as a pestle.)

Cold starters

Mimosa eggs 34
Stuffed eggs 34
Potted cheese 35
Terrine de lapin (Galantine of rabbit) 35
Liver pâté 36
Marinated kipper fillets 36
Danish smoked eel sandwich 37
Prawns in savoury jelly 38

Mimosa eggs

Serves 6

6 hard-boiled eggs
½ pint mayonnaise (page 129)
Lemon juice
A little cream

1 tbsp chopped chives
  or parsley
Watercress

Shell the eggs. Cut four of them in half lengthways and arrange in a serving dish. Cut the other two in half, remove the yolks and press the whites through a hair sieve.

Make a basic mayonnaise well spiked with lemon and mixed with a little cream to bring it to a coating consistency. Stir in the chives or parsley and coat the halved eggs.

Spoon small portions of the sieved egg whites between each egg and then press the yolks through a clean dry hair-sieve letting the mixture 'rain' over the coated eggs. Add bunches of watercress for garnish.

Stuffed eggs

Serves 8

8 hard-boiled eggs
2 oz softened butter
1 tbsp stiff mayonnaise
2 oz tuna fish (or sardines or
  pilchards)
1 tsp French-type mustard

1 tsp lemon juice
1 oz lumpfish roe (optional)
Salt and freshly milled pepper
8 stuffed olives, halved

Boil the eggs from cold for ten minutes (this way the whites will stay soft and not be rubbery). Cool under running cold water. Shell and cut in half lengthways. Mash the yolks together with the rest of the ingredients except the roe and halved olives. Fork the filling into the empty shells – or use a large star nozzle in a piping bag (if you do use this, it is better to liquidise all the ingredients then lumps don't block the nozzle).

Top each half egg with a cluster of lumpfish roe and a couple of halves of stuffed olive.

Potted cheese
Serves 4

2 oz farmhouse Cheshire
  cheese
2 oz unsalted butter
1 tbsp cream sherry or port

Pinch of cayenne pepper
1 tsp Worcester sauce
Clarified butter

Soften but do not melt the unsalted butter. Grate the cheese.
Combine these together with all the other ingredients, except the
clarified butter and pound them until you have a smooth paste.
(Remember, cayenne pepper is very hot.)

Press into little pots or wax cartons and cover with a film of
clarified butter.

This potted cheese is excellent as a stuffing for halved, peeled
pears which have been rubbed over with lemon juice to keep
them white. Serve as a first course or with a salad for lunch.

Terrine de lapin (Galantine of rabbit)
Serves 10 to 12

1 rabbit
2 lb loin or leg of pork
1 lb extra pork fat
5–6 chicken livers
¼ lb back bacon, diced
8 fl. oz rosé wine (or dryish
  white wine)
1 beaten egg

1 clove garlic
1 tsp ground ginger
3 tbsp Jamaican rum
Salt
Freshly-ground pepper
¾ lb streaky bacon to line dish
  (optional)

Bone the rabbit keeping the two back fillets whole. Cut these into
½ inch cubes and put to marinate together with the trimmed
chicken livers also cut into cubes, in the rum.

Put the leg or loin of pork and rabbit leg meat to marinate in
the wine with the garlic clove overnight. Next day mince the
meats from the wine marinade with the pork fat on the coarse
blade of a mincer. Mix in the wine marinade, ginger, diced fillet
and chicken livers.

Crush the clove of garlic and mix this in too adding the rum
juices, beaten egg and bacon. Season well with salt and pepper.
Pack into a terrine or seamless loaf tin, lined with bacon if liked
and cover with buttered foil.

Stand this in a second container of hot water (*bain-marie*) and bake at gas mark 4, 350°F (180°C), for 2 hours.

Remove the foil half an hour before the end of the cooking time. A terrine or pâté is cooked when the juices look quite clear. Cool the terrine before pressing with a weight and refrigerating. Serve in ½ inch-thick slices with hot toast or French bread.

Liver pâté

Serves 15 to 20

1½ lb pig's liver
1 lb pig's fat
2 small eggs
6 anchovy fillets

1 tsp ginger
¼ tsp powdered cloves
½ pint thick Béchamel sauce
 (page 117)

Mince the liver and anchovies twice, and put into a bowl. Mince the fat and render in oven or in a pan on top. Strain and leave to cool but not to set. Make up the white sauce and season. Beat eggs into liver. Stir this into white sauce. Beat in the strained rendered fat. Season well with salt, pepper and all the ginger and cloves. Cook covered in a terrine, in a water bath at gas mark 5, 375°F (190°C) for 1 hour. Cool, then refrigerate.

Marinated kipper fillets

Serves 4

4 uncooked kippers (2 pairs)

Marinade
1 level tbsp bland nut-oil
1 tbsp red or white wine
 vinegar

1 tbsp finely chopped onion
1 dsp finely chopped parsley

To serve
Rye bread fingers

Chopped parsley

Using your fingers and a very sharp, thin-bladed knife, carefully skin and fillet the kippers. Cut each fillet diagonally into six or seven strips, following the natural grain of the fish.

Put the onion and parsley into a screw-top jar with the oil and vinegar and shake until blended, pour into a dish. Put the strips of kippers into the marinade, cover with foil, chill and marinate for at least 3 hours. You could also marinate the kippers in French dressing (page 133).

Serve with a little extra freshly chopped parsley on top and buttered rye bread fingers.

Danish smoked eel sandwich

Serves 4

This was one of my favourite *smorrebrod* when I was living in Copenhagen. Use the larger Danish or Dutch eels: if these are not available then mini-eels or even tinned ones will do.

4 slices Danish rye bread or German *Vollkornbrot*
2 oz butter
1 level tsp mild French mustard

Squeeze of lemon juice
4 pieces of smoked eel cut the same length as the bread

Savoury Custard
¼ pint milk
2 whole eggs

1 extra egg white
Salt and milled pepper

Snipped chives or chopped parsley

Lemon wedges

First make the savoury custard. Beat the eggs and white, season, pour over the milk.

Butter a small oblong or square seamless tin or mould (a foil freezer container is ideal). Pour in the mixture. Stand the receptacle in a pan of cold water. Bring to the boil. Simmer until set and quite firm. Turn out and cut into suitable lengths for garnishing.

Then, cream the butter and mustard. Add a squeeze of lemon juice. Spread four slices of the rye bread liberally.

Skin and trim the eel. Arrange on top of the bread. Decorate with a slice of the cold egg custard and lemon wedges, and sprinkle with the chives or fresh parsley.

Eat as a light main course for lunch, and, although this is called a sandwich, it is eaten using a knife and fork.

Prawns in savoury jelly

Serves 4

Ideally this should have a jelly made from fish bones, but these days a short cut is more welcome.

4 oz shelled fresh or frozen
   prawns
4 inch piece of cucumber

Fennel fronds, dill weed or
   parsley
4 sprigs of parsley

For the jelly
½ oz aspic crystals
¼ oz gelatine crystals
¼ pint white wine

¾ pint water
Lemon juice
Salt to taste

Just how many prawns you use for each serving will depend on the state of the housekeeping!

Peel, deseed and cube the cucumber. Make up the jelly by dissolving the two crystals in hot water then adding the cold wine and seasoning. Pour a little of this into individual glasses and put them in the refrigerator to set. Now add a mixture of prawns and cucumber and chopped chosen herb. Add more jelly and chill again and continue like this until the glasses are filled. Top each glass with a sprig of parsley; a swirl of sour cream can add an interesting touch but is entirely optional.

Main courses

Ragoo of beef in beer 41
Beef in red wine (Boeuf Bourguignonne) 41
Dobe of beef (Dob'd beef) 42
Beef en daube Borderlaise (Beef in red wine jelly) 43
Minced beef cobbler pie 44
Beef, ham and chive mould 45
Collops of beef with pickled walnuts 46
Steak with green peppercorn sauce 46
Spaghetti Bolognese 47
Grilled hamburgers 48
Cheese burger 48
Spinach burger 48
Blue cheese burger 49

Lemon and herb stuffed lamb 49
Cutlets Reform 50
Roast saddle of Southdown lamb or Guard of Honour 51
Forcemeat balls 52
Kebob'd lamb 53
Gigot 'qui pleure' ('Weeping' lamb) 53
Devill'd kidneys 54

Elizabethan pork 55
Baked spiced ham 56
The Smith burger 56
Danish meatballs (Frikadeller) with red cabbage 57
Marbl'd veal 58

Boil'd capon 59
Silvered chicken Elizabeth II 59
Stuffed boned capon 60
Chicken and leek pie 61
'A blanket of fowl in cowcumbers' 62

Ragoo of beef in beer

Serves 6

1½lbs braising steak (in one thick piece)	1 level tsp powdered thyme
½ lb small onions	1 level tsp powdered bay leaf or 12 juniper berries
¾ lb large carrots	1 pint strong ale
¼ lb button mushrooms	Olive oil for frying
2 cloves garlic, crushed	Salt and freshly milled pepper
1 oz plain flour	Parsley
2 rashers streaky bacon	

Cut meat into large cubes (approximately 2 inches). Quarter the onions, then cut into eighths. Cut the carrots into sticks and quarter the mushrooms. Cut the bacon into striplets. Mix flour with herbs, salt and pepper. Dredge meat in flour, shake surplus off. Heat a little oil in a frying pan and brown the pieces of meat on all sides a few at a time. Remove from pan and put on one side whilst you fry the bacon, onions, carrots and mushrooms until lightly golden. Add garlic.

Transfer all the ingredients to an ovenproof pot. Shake over the surplus flour and cover with the beer. Cook at gas mark 3, 325°F (170°C) for up to 2 hours, or until the meat is quite tender.

Remove any excess fat from the surface of the braise, sprinkle liberally with freshly chopped parsley or any other green herbs, and serve with riced (mashed), creamed or new potatoes and a good light Yorkshire Pudding.

Beef in red wine (Boeuf Bourguignonne)

Serves 6

2 lb rump or braising steak	3 cloves garlic
Basic marinade (page 133)	4 oz button mushrooms
½ bottle red wine	1 oz butter
2 tbsp olive oil	1 bay leaf
8 oz button onions	1 sprig parsley
12 baby carrots	1 sprig thyme
8 oz piece of bacon	Salt and freshly milled pepper
1 oz flour	Chopped parsley

Cut the beef into sticks ½ inch by 1½ inches. Marinate in the Basic Marinade made with red wine. Leave overnight.

Drain and pat dry the meat, retaining the liquid.

Cut the bacon into sticks. Use whole baby carrots or cut larger carrots into even sticks.

Heat the oil and brown the bacon, then the carrots and then the onions, removing each to an ovenproof casserole as they are browned.

Now brown the beef, a little at a time, sprinkling with the flour and adding more oil if necessary. The oil will need to be smoking before each addition.

Bring the vegetables and meat together in the casserole, cover with the marinade and wine (making approximately 1 pint of liquid), season with the garlic, herbs, salt and pepper. Cover and cook in the oven, gas mark 3, 275°F (140°C), for 2½ hours to 3 hours. Quickly fry the white button mushrooms in the butter and add just before serving.

Sprinkle liberally with chopped parsley.

Dobe of beef (Dob'd beef)

Serves 6

This is based on a Tudor recipe.

2 lb best rump steak	6 cloves
4 oz fat pork or bacon	2 oz butter
2 carrots	1 pint strong ale or port
2 onions	1 oz flour
2 cloves garlic	1 tsp grated orange rind
½ stick celery	½ pint strong stock
½ tsp thyme	Salt and freshly ground black
½ tsp marjoram	pepper

Garnish

4 oz button mushrooms	1 tbsp freshly chopped parsley
8 artichoke bottoms (tinned)	2 oz butter
4 cooked new potatoes	Lemon segments
1 cooked carrot	

Trim the meat of the skin and fat and cut into 1 inch cubes. Cut the bacon or pork into ¼ inch dice. Cut all the vegetables into ½ inch dice. Put the meat and vegetables, together with the garlic, cloves and orange rind, into a dish and cover with the ale or port.

Sprinkle with the freshly chopped herbs (if dried ones are used, these should be tied in a muslin bag and put into the dobe with the vegetables). Leave the meat to marinate for 4 to 5 hours, overnight, or longer.

Drain the meat cubes and the vegetables, retaining the liquor. Melt the 2 oz of butter in a heavy-bottomed pan and when it has acquired a nice nutty flavour, brown the bacon in it, add the meat cubes and fry at a high temperature until the meat is sealed. This will be best done if you fry a little at a time.

Add the vegetables and the dried herbs if these are being used. Sprinkle with the flour, stir well in and cover with the marinade and the stock. Lightly salt and pepper, remembering that the sauce will be well reduced and therefore strong.

Transfer all the contents of the pan to an earthenware casserole and cover tightly, sealing the lid with a flour and water paste. Cook in the oven at gas mark 3, 275°F (140°C), for 5 hours. The finished dish should be a strongly flavoured, cohered mass.

For the garnish, cut and dice all the vegetables and toss them in the butter until they are thoroughly heated through. Season lightly. Drain and arrange attractively on top of the dobe just before serving.

Sprinkle with freshly chopped parsley and serve with the lemon segments in a side dish.

Plain riced potatoes are perfect with a rich dobe – a potato ricer (masher) is a piece of equipment well worth having.

Boeuf en daube Bordelaise (Beef in red wine jelly)

Serves 6 to 8

This way of cooking rump steak is ideal for a picnic, summer supper or a men-only lunch. It is eaten, of course, cold.

3–4 lb piece rump steak
1 bottle red Bordeaux wine (Claret)
1 tbsp wine vinegar
Bouquet garni
2 sprigs fresh tarragon or level tsp dried tarragon

4 cloves garlic, peeled and halved
6 oz fat salt pork, diced
1 oz butter
8 oz button or pickling onions
2 fl oz Cognac or Armagnac
Salt and pepper

Place the rump steak (trimmed of excess fat) into a large flat dish, season with salt and pepper.

Pour over the wine, vinegar, garlic halves, tarragon and bouquet garni. Leave to marinate for 24 hours turning the meat every two hours throughout the day.

Next day, remove the steak, drain and pat dry with paper towels. Heat a large frying pan, melt the butter, add the diced salt pork and onions and fry until lightly golden. Remove these with a draining spoon and set aside whilst you brown the steak well on both sides.

Transfer everything to a large lidded pan or ovenproof casserole, cover with the marinade and Armagnac or Cognac. Cook in the oven for 5 hours at gas mark 3, 325°F (170°C).

Then check the seasoning. Remove the meat. Slice it thinly and arrange on a large shallow platter (check to see that it will fit in your refrigerator, if not then use two smaller ones as the meat should be arranged in one layer, only slightly overlapping).

Strain the cooking liquor over the meat and refrigerate. The juices should set over the meat.

Minced beef cobbler pie

Serves 8 to 10

I have always been fond of savoury mince pie. I also like a 'cobbler'! Here I have combined the two, making a hearty dish for an impromptu Sunday lunch party. It is a rich filling which should only be made with best mince (you will notice I call for minced rump or braising steak). The light suet crust removes the need for potatoes – in fact the ubiquitous tossed green salad is all you need serve. The mince mixture freezes. The topping doesn't – at least, I haven't tried it.

Base
6 oz shortcrust pastry

Filling

2 fl oz oil (or butter and oil)	4 oz tomato purée
1 onion, finely chopped	1 oz plain flour
4 middle sticks celery, finely chopped	Salt, pepper and nutmeg
	Half bottle red wine
1 clove garlic, crushed	6 oz mushrooms, sliced
2 lb rump steak, minced	

Cobbler topping

6 oz self-raising flour	Salt and pepper
3 oz suet	1 whole egg, beaten with 2–3
1 tbsp chopped parsley	tbsp of cold water
1 level tbsp chopped chives	

The day before: heat a little of the oil in an enamelled iron or steel oven pot. Fry the onion and celery until lightly browned and soft. Add the garlic and continue frying for a minute or two. Remove. Fry the mince in batches over a good heat for a minute or two. Mix in the celery, onion and garlic. Stir in the tomato purée, then the flour. Lower the heat and let all this take on a little colour. Season with salt, pepper and nutmeg.

Remove the meat mixture to a dish. Deglaze the pot with the red wine, working all the brown residue into the wine with a wooden spatula. Return the mince to the pot. Add the sliced mushrooms. Mix all together well. Cover with a lid. Cook in the oven at gas mark 4, 350°F (180°C) for an hour.

Remove the lid. Check the seasoning. Skim off any fat on the surface and leave to cool overnight.

On the day: line an 8–9 inch diameter, 2 inch deep, loose-bottomed tin with the pastry. Fill with the mince mixture.

Toss all the dry ingredients for the topping together. Mix to a soft dough with the egg and water.

Press or roll out to ½ inch thickness. Cut 2 inch discs with a scone cutter or glass, and arrange on top of the meat, slightly overlapping, forming a circle.

Bake at gas mark 7, 425°F (220°C) for 25 minutes or until the cobbler top is risen and baked through.

Beef, ham and chive mould

Serves 8

¾ lb lean minced beef	3 tbsp cold water
¾ lb fat gammon rasher, minced	Salt, milled pepper
4 slices white bread, crumbed	1 heaped tbsp finely chopped chives (or parsley)
2 eggs	

Combine all ingredients and mix well together. Put into buttered seamless loaf tin or basin, and either steam (cover with buttered foil) for 2 hours, or bake in the oven in a water bath for 1½ hours at gas mark 5, 375°F (190°C). The former cooking method gives a pale coloured moist textured mould, the latter a somewhat darker drier finish – different but both good.

Collops of beef with pickled walnuts
Serves 4

Allow 2 thin pieces of beef fillet per serving (approximately 1 lb trimmed weight for 4 people).

1 lb beef fillet, sliced	¼ pint beef stock
2 oz butter	(from stock cube)
1 small onion, finely sliced	4 pickled walnuts
1 level tsp tomato purée	Scant tbsp of pickle liquor
1 level tsp flour	Salt and pepper
Sherry-glass Madeira	
(or sweet sherry)	

Heat the butter in a heavy-bottomed frying pan until nearly brown. Quickly fry the slices of fillet on both sides and remove to a warm serving dish. Add the onion to the pan and cook to golden brown. Stir in the purée and flour. Reduce the heat and, stirring all the time, let this take on some colour. Pour in the wine and pickle liquor and stock. Boil rapidly until well reduced.

Chop the walnuts and scatter over meat. Strain hot sauce over this and serve immediately.

Steak with green peppercorn sauce
Serves 4

4 fillet steaks	2 tbsp cream
A knob of butter	¼ pint Basic brown sauce
2 tbsp olive oil	(page 121)
Salt and pepper	1 tbsp green peppercorns
2 tbsp brandy	(in brine)

Trim the fillets of all fat and skin. Heat the oil in a frying pan, add the knob of butter. When the fat is hot and foaming fry the steaks to suit your taste. Season lightly after frying.

Remove steaks to a warm serving dish. Pour away all but one tablespoon of the pan juices. Pour in the brandy, ignite and whilst the alcohol is burning away add the Basic brown sauce and cream. Let the sauce bubble for a minute until all is smooth. (If it shows signs of being oily add a spoonful of water or stock.)

Season carefully with salt only. Strain into a little pan, re-heat, add the peppercorns and pour the hot sauce over the waiting steaks.

Spaghetti Bolognese

Serves 6 to 8

¾ lb best stewing or rump
   steak, minced
2 oz onion
3 tbsp olive oil
3 oz tomato purée
1 oz flour

½ pint red wine
½ pint stock (from stock cube)
1 large clove of garlic
Salt and freshly ground black
   pepper

Strip the steak of fat and sinew (I always use rump which is a little more expensive but has an excellent flavour). In areas where fat-free mince is available this is also good for this dish. Put the meat through a mincer twice.

In a heavy-bottomed pan fry the finely chopped onion in the oil until golden brown. Gradually add the minced meat, stirring well over a good heat until the meat browns. Now reduce the heat and add the tomato purée, taking care to work it well in and see that it does not burn. Sprinkle the flour over and mix well in.

Now – and here is the secret of a good brown sauce – over a low heat gradually allow a crust to form on the bottom of the pan. This should take about 10 minutes, but watch it carefully.

Remove the mixture to a large dinner plate. Turn up the heat again and pour in the red wine. With a wooden spatula work all this crust into a sauce. When the bottom of the pan is quite clear, replace the meat mixture into the winey sauce, add the crushed and chopped garlic and the stock and simmer for 30 minutes. Season lightly, bearing in mind that the stock cube already contains salt.

Serve with spaghetti or any other pasta.

Grilled hamburgers

Serves 2 or 3

12 oz lean best steak, minced
½ oz butter
1 tsp Worcester sauce
1 tsp lemon juice

1 tsp freshly chopped parsley (optional)
Salt and freshly milled pepper

Contrary to popular belief, a good hamburger does not have onion in the mixture. Shape the beef into two or three large round patties. Do not use flour. Do not bind with egg. Either grill on a fiercely hot charcoal grill, or under a pre-heated, very hot domestic grill, or – and I find this best – heat a heavy-bottomed skillet. Lightly sprinkle the surface with salt and fry the hamburgers to the desired degree: rare, medium, well-done.

Now brush with butter and sprinkle with lemon juice, parsley, Worcester sauce etc. before slotting between a split, warmed bread bun. (Do not butter the buns for hamburgers.) Then add any one, or even all, of the following garnishes.

Sliced onions, butter-fried until soft and golden-brown
Slices of skinned tomato
Slices of dill pickle (large gherkins in a mild, sweet vinegar)
Crisp lettuce leaves
Blobs of thick home-made mayonnaise (page 129)
Cole slaw
Hot creamed sweetcorn
Tomato ketchup and/or French mustard

Cheese burger

After grilling or frying, top each hamburger with a slice of melting cheese, and place under the grill until hot and bubbling. Transfer into a hot bun.

Spinach burger

Cook a packet of leaf spinach and drain well, pressing all the juice away. Combine with the minced meat. Season with nutmeg or mace. Fry as normal. Top with cheese. The bread buns may be toasted on the insides to gain a different effect.

Blue Cheese burger

Serves 4

Make a paste: 4 oz blue cheese (Stilton, Roquefort or Danish Blue), 2 oz butter, 1 tablespoon of chopped chives, juice of half small lemon, 2 teaspoons Worcester sauce or Yorkshire relish.

Make up eight thin beef patties, using 1½ lb of mince. Put a knob of the cheese mixture in the centre of four of these. Brush round the border with beaten egg, press the other four beef patties on top. Chill for 2 hours, then fry or grill as before. Any remaining cheese filling can be melted and poured over the finished hamburger before topping with the bun lid.

Lemon and herb-stuffed lamb

Serves 4

Lamb is a great favourite in Britain and some of the best lamb in the world comes from Wales and Suffolk. This delicate stuffing complements the sweet taste of the meat. Lemon was much used in the seventeenth and eighteenth centuries, as was garlic and all the lovely green herbs first grown in the Tudor herb gardens.

Leg or shoulder of lamb

Stuffing
4 oz fresh white breadcrumbs
2 oz butter or suet
1 small onion, chopped
1 clove garlic crushed
1 beaten egg
Salt and pepper
1 level tbsp each of fresh
 chopped parsley, chives,
 basil, thyme

Finely shredded rind of one
 small lemon
Juice of half this lemon

Melt the butter in a pan and soften the onion without letting it take any colour. Add the rest of the stuffing ingredients and bind with the egg. If dried herbs are used, you will have to be more discerning and I suggest you start with a teaspoon of each cutting down on the thyme somewhat. Stuff the meat in the usual way if boned, or make stuffing into forcemeat balls and roast round the meat or fry in a separate pan in butter.

Cutlets reform

Serves 4

Based on Charles Elmé Francatelli's recipe he created for London's famous Reform Club in the 19th century. Allow 2 lamb cutlets per person.

8 lamb cutlets
2 oz cooked minced ham
2 oz fresh white breadcrumbs

Oil and butter for frying
Seasoned plain flour
Seasoned beaten egg

Reform Sauce
1 small carrot, diced
1 small onion, chopped
2 rashers streaky bacon
1 oz butter or 2 tbsp oil
1 clove garlic, crushed
½ tsp dried thyme
6 whole allspice or cloves

4 tbsps white wine or cider vinegar
4 oz redcurrant jelly
Scant ¾ oz plain flour
¾ pint stock (use stock cube)
Salt and pepper
Gravy browning (natural colouring)

Garnish
2 oz cooked ham
1 large cooked carrot
2 gherkins

1 hard-boiled egg white
2 raw mushrooms

For the sauce, melt butter and fry bacon (cut into strips), carrots and onions until golden brown. Stir in flour, allow to brown lightly, add the vinegar, stock, redcurrant jelly and seasonings, salting carefully. Simmer for 30 minutes. Strain into a second pan and add brown colouring. Cut the garnish (known as Reform chips) into strips of equal size and add to sauce.

Trim the cutlets of the bulk of their fat. Trim the first inch of the bone clean. Dip each cutlet into seasoned flour, then into beaten egg, and finally press in the minced ham and crumbs mixed together. Fry in hot oil into which you have put a knob of butter for flavour. Three minutes on each side will leave the cutlets pink: fry longer if you wish them well done. Drain and serve on a dish paper with the reheated sauce.

Roast saddle of Southdown lamb or Guard of Honour

The saddle is an old English roast which is usually far too large for most modern ovens as it is virtually what it says it is; the saddle of the animal; the entire top end; neck, and loin right down to the kidneys.

An excellent alternative, when a party piece is called for, is a Guard of Honour where two best ends of loin of lamb have their bones trimmed clean of all fat and meat so that they can be interlocked, thus looking like the crossed swords of a military guard on some ceremonial occasion.

Lamb   Powdered rosemary
Softened butter   Garlic, crushed
Salt and pepper

To roast either the saddle or the Guard of Honour prepare in this way: rub a mixture of softened butter, salt, pepper, powdered rosemary and crushed garlic into the scored skin of the lamb, not forgetting to rub a little on the underside so that the meat is well aromatised. Stand the 'guard' on a rack and roast at a pretty high temperature, gas mark 9, 475°F (240°C), for 30 minutes then add 5 minutes per pound for rosé meat and 10 minutes for the meat to be more well done. For the saddle start the roasting at gas mark 9, 475°F (240°C) for the first 30 minutes, then reduce the heat to gas mark 4, 350°F (180°C) allowing 30 minutes to the pound for fairly well roasted meat. Those who prefer their lamb pink, allow only 15 minutes to the pound after the initial start.

To make a little gravy, drain away all but 2 tablespoons of the roasting fat then sprinkle in a heaped teaspoon of flour and ¾ piece of stock cube; stir all this together, add a glass of sherry and ½ pint of water. Bring to the boil, simmer for 15 minutes, strain into a heated sauce boat and serve.

The 'guard' is cut into cutlets for serving so ask your butcher to chine the loins so that it is easy to make the last cut through the bottom bone. Each bone end can be tipped with a cutlet frill, or a fancy flower fashioned out of foil to give a festive appearance. Serve with Forcemeat balls (page 52).

Forcemeat balls

Serves 5 or 6

4 oz fresh white breadcrumbs
3 oz suet
2 tbsp chopped parsley
1 tsp lemon rind
1 tbsp lemon juice
Butter
1 tsp dried rosemary

1 clove garlic
1 oz onion
2 eggs
Salt and freshly milled
    black pepper
Flour

Crush and fry the garlic with the finely chopped onion in a little butter.

Combine all the ingredients, except the flour. Form into 1½ inch diameter balls. Roll in flour and roast around the meat for the last 40 minutes of the roasting time, turning them halfway through their cooking time.

Kebob'd lamb

Serves 8

This is very spicy and hot and good!

3 lb leg of lamb

Marinade
3 tbsp yoghurt
1 tbsp tomato purée
1 tsp English mustard
2 tbsp olive oil
2 tbsp lemon juice
1 heaped tsp powdered
    coriander
½ tsp powdered clove
    (or cinnamon)

1 heaped tsp turmeric
½ tsp powdered mace
    (or nutmeg)
5 cloves garlic, crushed
1 large piece stem ginger,
    finely chopped
    (or ½ tsp powdered)
1 tsp salt
1 tsp cracked black pepper

Trim the skin and fat from the lamb and cut into 1 inch cubes. Make a few slits in each cube so the marinade gets well inside.

Put all the marinade ingredients into a blender to make a smooth paste.

Turn the lamb cubes in this mixture (in a china or glass bowl):

leave for 4 hours to marinade (or overnight), turning the pieces from time to time.

Oil some metal skewers and spear four or five cubes of meat per person. Grill for 5 minutes on each side, basting with any spare marinade as you go along (have the skewers 4 to 5 inches away from the heat).

With a fork, push the lamb cubes off the skewers onto a portion of 'pillow' rice. Garnish with raw onion rings. Serve with sticks of raw vegetables in a bowl of iced water to keep them crisp.

Gigot 'qui pleure' ('Weeping' lamb)
Serves 8

This is such a simple and effective way of cooking lamb I cannot think why we don't prepare it more often. In some way the idea is akin to the old Yorkshire method of roasting beef where the dripping falls into the pudding batter, which is cooked underneath the beef.

But, when cooking *Gigot 'qui pleure'*, the meat must be top quality as must the oil and butter. I do urge you to use olive oil for this (even chemists' olive oil is better than some corn oils).

6 lb leg of lamb (*see* Method)	Salt
2 tbsp olive oil	Freshly milled pepper
2 oz butter softened	6 medium potatoes
2 large cloves garlic	4 medium onions
Level tsp each of powdered thyme and bay leaf or thyme and rosemary	¾ pint stock (from stock cube)

Ask your butcher if he will prepare the leg of lamb in the French way which means taking out the 'step' bone only and leaving the shank whole. (We in Britain break the shank which means there is nothing to hold on to when carving.)

Slice each clove of garlic into 6 or 8 slivers. Then using a small, sharp pointed knife, plunge this into the flesh at 2 inch intervals and about 1½ inches deep across and down the leg on the top side.

Pressing the flesh open with the knife blade slide a sliver of garlic right into the small cavity, remove the blade and make the next incision. (If you like a lot of garlic you can insert more on the underside of the leg.)

Rub the butter all over the leg and rub in the herbs. Stand the leg in a roasting tin or an enamelled iron baking pan, spoon over the oil and start roasting it in a pre-heated oven at gas mark 8, 450°F (230°C), for half an hour.

Meanwhile peel and finely slice the potatoes and onions. Dissolve the stock cube in the ¾ pint of boiling water. Mix the onions and potatoes well together in a large bowl seasoning lightly with salt and pepper (and more chopped garlic if you like).

After the initial half hour take the leg from the oven and remove it whilst you layer the potatoes and onions in the fats in the roasting tin. Now pour over the stock.

Return the tin to the oven on a lowish shelf. Slide in the next shelf immediately over the tin and arrange the leg over this so that the juices will drip (weep) into the potatoes.

Continue to roast the lamb for a further hour (or more if you like it very well done). Depending on the size and type of oven you may have to reduce the temperature a notch or two if it starts to burn. But you should have a good roasting noise going on!

I serve my *Gigot 'qui pleure'* with a tossed salad and some English shaken pease (see page 101). No gravy. No Mint sauce, though I have been known to offer apple or sage jelly.

Devill'd kidneys

2 lamb kidneys per person	Melted butter or oil

Devil butter (for 4 kidneys)

4 oz butter, softened	½ tsp milled black pepper
1 tsp curry paste	½ tsp mustard powder
Pinch of cayenne pepper	1 tsp paprika
Salt	1 tsp Worcestershire sauce

Blend all the Devil Butter ingredients together, using a flexible palette knife and a large dinner plate (or directly on a work surface). Chill. Serve the grilled kidneys topped with butter.

Skin and trim the kidneys. Brush with melted butter or oil, and grill or fry in the usual way.

Devil Butter is also excellent with grilled chicken, chops and sausages, but remember it is very hot.

Elizabethan pork
Serves 12

As the fork was not really in vogue during Tudor times many dishes were served in 'ragoo' form so that they were easily eaten with a spoon. This dish is beautifully spicy, which suits today's palate. Ideal for buffet parties and also for the freezer; it is also better for making a day or so in advance. The quantities given here are for 12 persons or you can use one half and freeze the second for later use.

3 lb leg of pork (or veal)
Head of celery
2 onions
8 oz tin of apricots
6 oz seedless raisins
1 lemon
1 orange
6 oz stoned dates
2 large Cox's apples
1 tbsp clover honey

1 oz plain white flour
4 tbsp oil
½ bottle red wine or ½ pint cider or strong ale
1 level tsp each of: marjoram, thyme, cinnamon, mace, black pepper, mild curry powder
3 crushed cloves garlic
Salt and pepper

Garnish
4 segmented oranges
4 oz toasted walnuts

Butter

Trim the meat of any skin, bone and excess fat. Cut into ½ inch cubes and dredge in the seasoned flour. Heat some of the oil and fry the meat until lightly brown; this is best done a little at a time transferring the fried cubes with a draining spoon to an oven-proof casserole. Next brown the finely sliced onions and celery transferring these also to the pot.

Sprinkle over any remaining flour. Add the apricots, drained and roughly chopped; raisins (not sultanas); the juice and finely grated rind of the lemon and orange; the dates, roughly chopped; the apples, cored and roughly chopped; the honey, wine, garlic and herbs. Cover with a lid and cook in the oven at gas mark 3, 325°F (170°C) for 3 hours.

To serve, heat a good piece of butter in a frying pan and toss the walnuts in this until they are hot. Scatter these over the surface of the finished dish and decorate with pithless segments of orange. A good mealy jacket potato, plain fluffy rice or buttered noodles goes well with this rich Tudor stew.

Baked spiced ham

Serves 8

3–4 lb piece of gammon

Glaze

1 tbsp apricot purée (or sieved apricot jam)

1 tbsp clover honey

1 tsp dry mustard

1 tsp powdered cinnamon

1 tbsp wine or cider vinegar

To roast, cover the ham completely in foil and bake at gas mark 6, 400°F (200°C), allowing 20 minutes to the pound.

Three-quarters of an hour before the end of the cooking time take the ham from the oven, remove the skin, and score the fat in inch apart diagonal cuts. Make a paste with the glaze ingredients and spread this over the fat surface of the ham. Baste at 15 minute intervals for the rest of the cooking time so that a golden sweet glaze forms. This should be done in the oven at gas mark 5, 375°F (190°C).

If the ham is to be served hot, serve broad beans in a rich parsley sauce with it. If served cold then any attractive salad will suffice, but orange and tomato marries exceptionally well with it.

The Smith burger

Serves 8

Louis' in New Haven, Connecticut claims to be the originator of the hamburger in America back in the 1880s. Still in full swing today, this tiny family-run business uses the original nineteenth-century vertical gas grills for cooking and, more interestingly, the finished burger is served in toasted bread, not the soft pappy sesame roll we have come to expect. I, too, prefer mine in toast. Makes eight 3 inch burgers.

1 lb green gammon, coarsely minced

1 lb white raw chicken meat, coarsely minced

Salt and white pepper

Pinch of mace

16 slices of toast, cut into rounds with a large pastry cutter, buttered or dry

Mix the meats together. Form into patties with wetted hand. Season well. Grill or pan-fry the burgers. Put between the toast and serve with extra relishes of your choice: tomato sauce, apple chutney, sweetcorn.

Danish meatballs (Frikadeller) with red cabbage
Serves 4 or 5 (12–15 meatballs)

¾ pint milk
3½ oz flour
1½ lb minced lean pork (or pork and veal)
2 egg whites, or 1 whole egg

1 medium onion, grated
2 tsp salt
Freshly milled white pepper
Butter for frying (about 4 oz)

Make a well in the flour and gradually mix it to a smooth batter with the milk. Add the onion, then work this into the minced meat. Beat in the egg whites. Season well, and leave the mixture to stand for 1 hour before frying the meatballs.

Melt half the butter in a frying-pan until foaming and just turning brown (an essential state for a good nutty flavour). Dip a tablespoon into the hot butter and 'draw' egg-shaped mounds of the mixture from the bowl until the pan is two-thirds full. Fry for 8 to 10 minutes, turning and moving the Frikadeller about. Drain well. Serve warm, with crisp-fried onions, on buttered rye bread with red cabbage on top and potato salad in a lettuce leaf. Serve cold, cut into slices.

Red cabbage
1 lb red cabbage, finely sliced
1 large baking apple, peeled and sliced
1 onion peeled and sliced and fried in an ounce of butter

⅛ pint red wine vinegar
⅛ pint water
2 tbsp redcurrant jelly
1 oz brown sugar
Salt and pepper

Bring all the ingredients together except the jelly. Simmer on top or in a moderate oven for 1½ hours, or until all is homogeneous. Stir in the redcurrant jelly and add more salt and pepper if necessary. Serve hot, warm or cold. This also goes well with roast pork, duckling, sausages or goose and also may be served as an interesting vegetable.

Marbl'd veal

Serves 8 to 10

As the name implies this dish has the look of marble when sliced and was just another way the Georgians had of making their foods look attractive and appetising. I see it as England's more-than-excellent answer to the French 'terrine'. It is essentially a party dish and can be served as a starter or as a main dish with salads. The quantities demanded to make a good dish warrant its use for about 8–10 people but it freezes well and keeps in the refrigerator for at least a week. In fact it is better for being made two or three days in advance. It must be served thinly sliced.

¾ lb fillet of veal
¾ lb fat pork
¼ lb extra pork fat
½ lb cooked ox tongue, bought in one piece
2 raw chicken breasts, skinned and boned
2 eggs, beaten
Shredded rind of one small lemon

2 tbsp freshly chopped parsley
1 tbsp finely chopped chives or green tops of spring onions
1 heaped tsp aspic crystals or gelatine
1 teacup Madeira (or cold water)
Salt and freshly milled pepper

Trim meat of gristle and skin. Put veal, pork and fat twice through mincer. Add seasonings and herbs and bind with beaten eggs. Cut tongue and chicken breasts into ½ inch cubes and mix with the minced meats. Warm Madeira or water and dissolve aspic crystals in this; work this well into the meats.

Butter or oil a seamless loaf tin or ovenproof pot large enough to contain the mixture. Fill the receptacle, cover with a lid or foil; stand in a second container such as a roasting tin with enough hot water to come half-way up the sides. Cook in pre-heated oven at gas mark 4, 350°F (180°C) for 1½ hours.

Cool before covering with a weight and chilling in the refrigerator to set.

Boil'd capon

Serves 5 or 6

This is still one of the best ways of eating chicken or capon. Make sure the stock is good and strong so that the sauce is rich and worthwhile.

3–5 lb capon
3 large carrots
2 large onions
½ head celery

2 crushed cloves garlic
1 fresh bay leaf
Salt and pepper
Water

Sauce
1–1½ pints stock from capon
1½ oz flour
3 oz good butter

¼ pint double cream
A little lemon juice

Select a pan which will just fit the capon (or chicken) with the peeled vegetables packed tightly around it. Cover with cold water, add the garlic, bay leaf and a little salt and simmer until just tender (about 1½ hours for a 5 lb bird). Skim carefully from time to time.

Skin the bird and cut into nice serving pieces, or bone it entirely, cutting the meat into fork-size pieces. Cut up the vegetables attractively.

Melt the butter in a saucepan, stir in the flour; add one pint of boiling strained stock. Stir until you have a smooth sauce. Add the cream and more stock if necessary, season carefully with salt, pepper and lemon juice. Strain again over the waiting chicken and serve with rice, creamed potatoes, noodles, or any form of pasta. It is a good idea to add just a modicum of yellow colouring to this sauce; it looks richer and creamier.

Silvered chicken Elizabeth II

Serves 4

I covered the breasts of the chicken with real edible silver leaf. Gold and silver leaf was often used in Elizabeth I's time for ornamenting foods. This was a delightful visual extravagance employed to link the two royal ladies. But as silver leaf is very costly, I suggest you cut a silver foil breastplate for the bird for decoration after roasting.

4 lb chicken

Stuffing	2 oz bacon
4 oz white breadcrumbs	1 oz butter
2 oz walnuts	½ tsp powdered mace
4 tomatoes	Salt and pepper
1 onion	1 beaten egg

Skin, seed and chop the tomatoes. Chop the onion and cut the bacon into fine strips. Crush the walnuts.

Soften the onion in the butter. Fry bacon until crisp. Combine rest of the ingredients, binding with the beaten egg.

Stuff the chicken at the neck end and roast at gas mark 6, 400°F (200°C), for 30 minutes per lb.

Stuffed boned capon

Serves 6

The capon can be prepared a day in advance.

6–7 lb capon, boned

Ham and brazil nut stuffing

1 lb piece of gammon, soaked overnight in cold water if necessary	Pepper
	4 oz brazil nuts, roughly chopped
1 oz butter	1 tsp tomato purée
1 small onion, finely chopped	1 tsp finely grated orange zest
4 oz fresh white breadcrumbs	1 egg, beaten
½ tsp ground mace	Extra butter
Salt and pepper	

To make the stuffing

Cut gammon into small pieces and fry in 1 oz butter for 2–3 minutes only. Turn the ham, but let it take on a little colour. Remove the ham pieces with a slotted spoon. Soften onion in the juices until transparent.

Put the pan ham and onion through the fine blade of a mincer. Mix with the rest of the ingredients and bind with the egg. No salt will be needed.

Form the stuffing into an oval shape. Turn the boned capon skin-side down on to a work surface. Spread it out whichever way it wants to go.

Place the stuffing on top of the breast meat. Then wrap, fold and tuck the leg and wing meat (and skin) round this, arriving at a nice shape.

Thread a bodkin with fine string or linen thread and approach the next step as if you were darning a badly torn and worn quilted dressing gown, darning, tucking and holding the seams together to hold in any stuffing or flesh. Sew and bind up.

Spread soft butter over the surface, seasoning with salt and pepper and ½ tsp of dried ground mace.

Stand the capon on a rack in a roasting tin. Cover the breast with 3 or 4 layers of butter muslin soaked in a little melted butter or a piece of buttered foil. Roast at gas mark 6, 400°F (200°C) for two hours, lowering the temperature to gas mark 4, 350°F (180°C) after an hour. Serve cut into handsome ½ inch thick slices, pour a ladle of the Tomato madeira sauce (page 126) round each slice.

Chicken and leek pie

Serves 5 or 6

4 oz shortcrust pastry
4 oz puff pastry
8 leeks, washed, trimmed and
  finely sliced
3–4 oz butter
Salt and pepper

Thick white sauce
½ pint milk infused with a
  piece of onion, bay leaf, and
  sprig of thyme

2 chicken breasts, about 12 oz
  in all, boned
½ tsp ground mace
1 dessertspoon soy sauce
  (optional)
1 egg, beaten

1 oz flour
1 oz butter

Butter a lipped 9–10 inch diameter, 1½ inch deep, loose-bottomed tin and line with the short-crust pastry.

Roll out the puff pastry and cut a lid to fit. Bake blind.

Make up thick white sauce: melt the butter, stir in the flour and gradually add the milk after infusing it with onion, bay leaf and thyme for 30 minutes over a low heat.

Soften the sliced leeks in 2 oz butter in a lidded pan, stirring occasionally. Check seasoning and set aside.

Cut the chicken breasts into ½ inch cubes. Season with salt and mace.

Melt 1 oz of butter in a large frying pan until it is lightly browned and foaming. Fry the chicken in two batches for a couple of minutes only. Add extra butter if necessary. Bring the fried chicken together, splash over the soy sauce and mix well, coating each bit lightly. Remove with a slotted spoon.

Mix the leeks with the white sauce. Mix in the chicken cubes, fill into the pie case and wet the edges. Fit the pastry lid. Brush with beaten egg, and decorate as desired. Bake at gas mark 7, 425°F (220°C) for 30 minutes until the pastry is puffed up, crisp and golden brown. Serve hot or cold.

'A blanket of fowl in cowcumbers'

Serves 4

Blanket is the early English spelling of the French word *blanquette*, meaning white. Cucumbers were frequently referred to as cowcumbers.

4 chicken breasts	¼ pint dry white wine, cider or stock
4 tomatoes	1 oz butter
½ cucumber	Salt and pepper
1 tbsp finely chopped shallot or onion	Extra butter
¼ pint thick cream	

Skin and bone the chicken breasts but leave the tip of the breastbone in. Melt the butter in a shallow pan until melted but not hot. Lay in the chicken breasts and 'poach' gently at the lowest heat for 2 minutes only on each side. Remove the breasts to a warm serving dish.

Skin, deseed and chop the tomatoes. Peel and deseed the cucumber and cut into half moons or dice. Add the shallot to the pan, raise the heat and simmer or sweat the shallot until tender. Add the chopped tomatoes, white wine and cream, and boil the whole until thick and viscous – this will take about 5 minutes.

In an extra knob of butter, simmer the cucumber until just tender but still somewhat crisp. Season lightly, and strain, adding the juices to the sauce whilst that is reducing. Season the sauce delicately at this stage – not earlier, as you may add too much for a sauce which is to be reduced.

Add the strained cucumber to the sauce, pour the whole over the waiting chicken breasts, and serve immediately.

Chicken creams in shrimp sauce

Serves 8

10 oz raw chicken breast when skinned and boned	2 eggs
½ pint double cream	Salt and pepper
	A touch of nutmeg

Sauce

4 oz fresh shrimps (or frozen in shells)	1 oz butter
1 baby onion	½ oz plain flour
½ pint boiling water	1 tsp lemon juice
¼ pint thick cream	1 tsp paprika
Clove garlic, crushed	1 level tsp tomato purée
	Salt and pepper

First prepare the sauce. Shell the shrimps and put them on one side; retain the heads and shells. Chop the onion and soften this in the melted butter in a small pan. Sprinkle with the flour and stir well in; add the paprika, garlic and purée. Pour on the boiling water and bring the sauce to the boil again. Add the cream and simmer for 2 minutes; add the shrimp shells and heads, cover the pan with a lid and, over the lowest possible heat, simmer the sauce for 20 minutes, stirring occasionally to prevent any sticking.

Strain the sauce through a fine sieve into a basin. Wash out the pan and return the sauce to it. Season with lemon juice, salt and pepper (it may be salty enough, so take care). Don't add the shrimps at this stage or they will toughen. Cover the surface of the sauce with a circle of buttered paper and stand the pan in a larger pan of hot water to keep warm.

Before making the chicken creams, make sure that you have a baking dish large enough to contain either castle pudding moulds or individual soufflé dishes. Failing this, small straight-sided coffee cups work very well – or the whole cream can be made in a ring mould. The quantity given will make eight creams in moulds which are about 2½ inches in diameter. Butter the moulds well.

Beat the eggs. Chill the cream in the refrigerator. Wipe the chicken, put first through the fine blade of the mincer and then, with the beaten eggs, through a blender or Mouli, making as fine a purée as you can. Chill this well and then gradually beat the cream little by little into the purée, adding a little salt if it looks as though it is getting too thin. You will notice that the mixture 'seizes' and thickens when you do this, but take care to be quite modest with the salt. Add a little pepper and nutmeg. When all the cream is incorporated, you should have a mixture which is just about dropping consistency.

Pre-heat the oven to gas mark 6, 400°F (200°C). Two-thirds fill the baking dish with hot water and place this on the centre shelf. Two-thirds fill the moulds, stand them in the water bath in the oven and bake for 25–30 minutes.

Have heated plates at the ready if you want the creams to be at their lightest, turn out the creams, coat each with sauce, to which you have added the shrimps, and serve at once.

Chicken in curry mayonnaise
Serves 8

1 capon or chicken

Sauce
½ pint Mayonnaise (page 129)   ½ pint Curry sauce (page 127)

Garnish
8 oz flaked almonds   Salt
1 oz butter   1 tin apricot halves

Boil or steam the chicken in the usual way. Reserve the stock for use in soups.

Cool, strip and bone the bird and cut the flesh into striplets or cut into serving-size pieces.

Mix the curry sauce and mayonnaise together, adjusting the consistency so that it just coats the chicken.

Pour sauce over the chicken pieces. Sprinkle with almonds which have been lightly browned in foaming butter, cooled and lightly salted.

Decorate with apricot halves (drained).

Tandoori style chicken
Serves 4

Strictly speaking, this Indian way of cooking chicken should be in a *tandoor*, a special clay oven that was at one time peculiar to the north-west frontier but is universally popular today. Also, small whole birds are considered the proper thing to use. However, since it is so good and simple to do, I have adapted a traditional recipe for regular household use, using an ordinary domestic grill. Of course, in the summer Tandoori Style Chicken is ideal for outside barbecuing, where the aroma of meat cooking makes a mouthwatering prelude to its delicious spicy flavour. The only ingredient I haven't included is fine weather.

4 large whole chicken breasts

Marinade

1 onion, chopped roughly
3 cloves garlic, crushed
1 small carton yoghurt
2 tbsp lemon juice
4 tbsp olive oil
1 tsp salt
½ tsp milled or cracked pepper
1 level tsp ground ginger
1 tsp turmeric
½ tsp mace or ¼ tsp nutmeg

1 heaped tsp ground coriander
1 tsp mild paprika
¼ tsp cayenne (hot) or 2 good dashes tabasco
1 level tsp garam masala
¼ tsp ground cinnamon
Orange, or a mixture of red and yellow colouring (optional)
Halved lemons for serving

Start the day before you want to serve the chicken. Whether or not you remove the chicken skin is up to you, but leave in the rib cage bones. Trim or snip off the wings as they get in the way when using a domestic grill. Make three or four deep incisions in the flesh, cutting diagonally across each breast to allow the marinade to get right into the flesh, and also to speed up the cooking process without drying out the meat.

Mix together all the ingredients for the marinade, pour over the chicken pieces and leave for 24 hours or overnight.

Preheat the grill to spanking hot. Brush the rack or pan with oil. Coat the chicken pieces with the marinade and place on the bars. Grill at a good heat for 5 to 6 minutes on each side. Lower the grill pan or, if outside, lift it a notch or two away from the heat source. Continue cooking for a further 10 to 12 minutes on each side, turning *frequently* and basting with a little of the marinade.

It is almost impossible to give even a nearly accurate cooking time as grills and barbecues vary so much in structure. If in doubt, use a sharp knife and cut into the *thick* part of the flesh and have a peek. Remember that chicken legs take longer.

Michael Smith's Coq au vin (Chicken in red wine)

Serves 4

1 roasting chicken (3–4 lb) cut in four large serving pieces; 2 legs, 2 breasts
2 oz lean belly pork, diced
1 medium onion, chopped
2 oz French butter
2 tbsp olive oil
2 cloves garlic, crushed
Freshly-chopped parsley and/or tarragon
Bouquet of herbs (stick of celery, 4 parsley stalks, sprig of thyme and 1 large bay leaf tied together)
1 sherry glass of brandy
Red wine to cover (Burgundy or Beaujolais)
2 oz tiny button mushrooms
Beurre-manié (page 13)
Salt and freshly-milled pepper

Melt the oil and butter together in a frying- or sauté pan just large enough to contain the chicken pieces. Brown the pork and onion. Remove these with a draining spoon and set aside whilst you fry the chicken pieces on all sides until a really good golden brown. (If you want your *Coq au Vin* to be even winier, the raw chicken portions can be soaked overnight in the red wine, before being drained and patted dry ready for frying.)

Pour over the brandy and set alight.

Pour in enough red wine to just cover the pieces, add the browned pork and onions, bouquet of herbs and garlic.

Season carefully with salt and milled pepper.

Simmer for 45 minutes, removing the breasts when they are cooked and leaving the thighs longer if necessary. When cooked remove the chicken to a warm lidded dish and keep hot.

Add the mushrooms to the liquid and simmer for 5 minutes during which time whisk in little bits of *beurre-manié* until the sauce is *lightly* thickened (just about as thick as single cream). Cook for 10 minutes.

Pour the sauce, unstrained, over the chicken pieces, sprinkle with freshly chopped parsley and/or tarragon and serve at once.

I prefer buttered noodles or dauphinois potatoes with *Coq au Vin*. If neither of these is your choice, then a lovely crisp-skinned floury baked potato is good for mopping up the rich red wine sauce.

A green salad should be served on a separate plate.

Poulet sauté au vin jaune (Sautéed chicken in jura wine)
Serves 4

This dish is a speciality of the mountainous Jura region of France near the borders of Switzerland where a special wine is grown in and around the town of Arbois. The wine is strong and yellow in colour, resembling a dry sherry in taste.

It is a simple dish to make consisting of chicken, yellow wine, rich cream and a handful of morilles if you can get them; if not, then mushrooms will do.

3 lb chicken, jointed	¼ pint dry white Bordeaux)
2 oz butter	¼ pint double cream
4 oz mushrooms	Salt and pepper
½ pint vin Jaune (or ¼ pint	*Beurre-manié* (page 13)
Amontillado Sherry and	

Cut the chicken into 4 serving pieces (2 legs and 2 breasts).

Melt the butter in a skillet or frying pan. Brown the pieces on all sides. Season lightly with salt and pepper.

Cover with a lid, reduce the heat and 'sweat' the chicken for 20 minutes. Remove the breasts to a warm platter.

Pour the wine over the legs and continue cooking for a further 10 minutes or until the legs are tender. Take these out and put with the breasts. Reduce the liquor by half by boiling rapidly. Add the sliced mushrooms and double cream to the pan and boil rapidly for a few minutes. If the sauce appears too thin (it should just coat the back of a wooden spoon) whisk in a tiny bit of *beurre-manié*.

Just before pouring over the waiting chicken pieces, stir in 1 further tablespoon of the vin Jaune or dry sherry. Serve with buttered noodles or rice pilaf and a tossed green salad.

Gâteau de foie de volaille sauce d'ecrevisses
(Hot chicken liver mousse with shrimp sauce)

Serves 5 to 6

1 dozen chicken livers
1 oz creamed butter
1 stock cube dissolved in 2
    tbsp boiling water
2 whole eggs

½ pint milk
2 egg yolks
Salt and pepper
Thin cream and milk (about ½
    pint altogether)

After skinning and trimming the livers soak them in the milk for at least an hour. Discard the liquid.

Cut the livers into pieces and liquidise with the softened butter, stock and whole eggs and egg yolks. Season carefully.

Add enough cream and milk to make a sloppy mixture. Pour into a buttered soufflé dish. Stand the dish in a pan of simmering water on top of the stove and cover with foil. Poach for 1½ hours without letting the water boil.

Shrimp sauce
½ lb shrimps or prawns in
    shells
½ pint single cream
Beurre-manié (page 13)

Drop lemon juice
1 tbsp whisky
¼ tsp mild paprika
Pepper

Shell the shrimps. Put the shells (heads and all) with the cream into a pan, add the paprika and whisky. Simmer with lid on for 20 minutes.

Strain the sauce into a smaller pan, discard the shells and whisk in a modicum of *beurre-manié* into the sauce until the sauce is very lightly thickened, about the consistency of single cream. (If too much sauce adheres to the shells, splash a little water over them in a basin, re-strain, then bring the sauce back to consistency by boiling rapidly for a minute or so.)

Season with lemon juice and a little pepper.

Add the shelled shrimps *just* before serving (they toughen if heated for too long).

Turn the mousse onto a warm serving platter, coat with the delicate shrimp sauce and serve with rice and salad.

Roast stuffed duckling

Serves 4

4 lb duckling

Stuffing

4 oz dried apricots, soaked overnight
2 oz split almonds
2 oz seedless raisins
1 medium onion
2 oz fresh white breadcrumbs
1 tsp grated orange rind
1 level tsp allspice
1 oz butter
1 tbsp sherry
1 tsp brown sugar
Salt and freshly milled black pepper
Dried sage

Chop onion and fry until golden brown in the butter. Cut the apricots into smallish pieces then mix all ingredients into a 'loose' stuffing. Stuff the duck in the usual way, rub butter and dried sage and salt into the skin. Roast 20 minutes to the pound at gas mark 5, 375°F (190°C).

Caneton aux Navets (Roast duckling with young turnips)

Serves 4 or 5

5 or 6 lb duck
2 lb young turnips
1 oz butter
½ tsp each rubbed sage, thyme, dry mustard
Salt and freshly milled pepper
2 tbsp castor sugar

Stuffing

Duck's liver
½ oz butter
1 oz onion, finely chopped
1 oz mushrooms, finely chopped
1 oz brown breadcrumbs
2 rashers bacon, finely diced
1 tbsp sherry or brandy
Salt and freshly milled pepper

Gravy

1 tsp flour
1 tsp tomato purée
½ chicken stock cube
Dry sherry
½ pint water

First make the stuffing by melting the small amount of butter in a small frying pan. Season. 'Set' the liver – by cooking it quickly on

69

both sides for ½ a minute or so. This will enable you to chop it into small pieces more easily. Fry the onion in the pan fats until transparent. Add the bacon and fry this, then add the mushrooms and continue frying everything for a couple of minutes, stirring all the time. Add the crumbs, chopped liver and sherry. Season. Leave this mixture to cool whilst you prepare the duck for the oven.

To do this, make a paste with the butter, herbs and seasonings. Rub this all over the duck's skin.

Stuff the duck with the prepared stuffing, stand it on a rack in a roasting tin and roast in a pre-heated oven gas mark 6, 400°F (200°C) for half an hour, then reduce the temperature to gas mark 4, 350°F (180°C), for a further hour or until the duck is done to your liking. If you like it well done then this could take up to 2 hours all told.

To make a little rich gravy

Pour away into a bowl all the duck fat from the roasting tin except 2 tablespoonfuls and leave any sediments in the tin. Sprinkle the flour into the tin, stir this round and, over a low heat, let this brown a little. Work in tomato purée and let this take on a little colour (but don't burn). Crumble in stock cube and add a sherry glass of dry sherry. Add cold water. Bring to the boil and transfer everything to a small pan. Leave to simmer for 15 minutes. Check the seasoning. Strain into a warm sauceboat and serve.

To prepare the turnips

Peel and wash them. Cut them into 2 inch-long even-sized batons. Par-boil them for 5 to 6 minutes in boiling salted water. Drain them on kitchen paper.

When the duck is ready strain 4 or 5 tablespoons of the retained roasting fats into a large frying pan. Add castor sugar and then, over a moderate heat, allow the sugar to caramelise, which it will do in the 'pool' of caramel now to be seen floating in the duck fat.

Add the well-drained turnips stirring them round so they acquire a coating of this caramel. Leave them to cook until tender, taking care they do not burn. Remove them with a draining spoon and serve them round the duck.

Duckling with orange sauce

Serves 4

1 duckling
½ tsp salt and black pepper

1 orange
  (juice and grated rind)
1 oz butter

Sauce
1 orange
  (juice and grated rind)

½ pint Basic brown sauce
2 tbsp brandy

Garnish
2 oranges, segmented

Watercress

Make a paste with the butter, finely grated rind of one orange, salt and pepper and rub this into the skin of the duckling. Roast at gas mark 5, 375°F (190°C), for 20 minutes to the pound. When the duckling is cooked, quarter or carve it and put into a warm serving dish.

Pour away all excess fat from the roasting tin. Pour in the brandy, blaze this, then add the brown sauce and juice of the two oranges. Reduce the sauce by boiling rapidly until it is bright and viscous. Season lightly if necessary. Strain into a smaller pan. Shred the orange rind and blanch in a little boiling water. Strain and add to the sauce.

Arrange orange segments over the cooked duckling and pour over the boiling sauce.

Decorate with bunches of crisp, lightly salted, watercress.

Lapin aux deux moutardes
(Braised rabbit in a two-mustard sauce)

Serves 4

1 English rabbit, sectioned or 2 packs Chinese frozen rabbit (which will yield 2 hind legs and 2 good back portions)
2 oz onions, sliced
2 oz white mushrooms, sliced
1 clove garlic, crushed
Small pinch dried thyme
¾ pint light chicken stock (using ½ a stock cube)
½ pint dry white wine
¼ pint thick cream
½ small tsp made English mustard
2 heaped tsp (or more) mild Dijon mustard
Beurre-manié (page 13)
Squeeze lemon juice
Salt and freshly milled white pepper
Butter and olive oil for frying
1 tbsp freshly chopped tarragon or parsley

Heat 2 tablespoons of olive oil and one ounce of butter in a heavy-bottomed sauté – or frying pan (with a lid which will be required later). When lightly smoking, brown the rabbit portions on all sides, turning them at intervals to ensure even colouring and always working with the pan over a good strong heat.

Remove the pieces to one side whilst you lightly brown the onions first and then the mushrooms in the same fats.

Return the rabbit to the pan in one layer. Season very lightly with salt and milled pepper (the stock cube and mustard contain salt). Add the crushed garlic and thyme. Pour the stock and wine over the rabbit. It should barely cover the pieces. Cover with a lid and gently simmer the rabbit until tender (about 30 minutes).

Remove the pieces to a warm serving dish. Strain the liquid into a second pan and reduce this by boiling rapidly until you have about ¾ pint left. Now, whisk in little bits of *beurre-manié* to thicken the sauce allowing it to boil well between each addition.

The sauce at this stage should be no thicker than single cream. Next, whisk in the two mustards, adding more French mustard if you like a good mustardy flavour. Pour in the thick cream and allow the sauce to boil rapidly for 2 to 3 minutes. Check seasoning adding a squeeze of lemon juice to 'lift' the flavours.

Strain the finished sauce over the waiting rabbit pieces. Sprinkle liberally with the tarragon, or parsley.

(This recipe can be made in exactly the same way, using chicken portions instead of rabbit.)

'Conyngs in Greke wyne'

Serves 4

This recipe is said to have been served at the coronation banquet of Henry IV. Conyng is the Old English word for rabbit.

1 rabbit, sectioned	4 oz tinned apricot halves
Seasoned flour	(when drained)
Oil for frying	3 pieces stem ginger, shredded
½ pint sweet Greek red wine	1 level tsp cinnamon
(or a sweet white wine)	1 level tsp powdered cloves
2 tbsp cider vinegar	12 juniper berries (optional)
4 oz muscatel raisins	Salt and milled pepper
4 oz sultanas	

Dredge the pieces of rabbit in well-seasoned flour and fry until golden brown in gently smoking oil. Drain away any excess oil. In a basin, have soaking all the other ingredients: wine, vinegar, spices and fruits. Pour these over the rabbit pieces, cover and simmer for 30–40 minutes or until the largest pieces are tender; remove the back fillets as soon as they are cooked (which will be first).

Remove the rest of the rabbit pieces and keep warm whilst you reduce the sauce until thick, by boiling rapidly for 10–15 minutes. Check seasoning. Serve with rice, riced (mashed) potatoes or noodles.

This dish is also excellent made with chicken portions instead of rabbit.

Quail with grapes

Serves 2

4 quail	Rosemary, finely chopped
1 oz butter	4 tiny butter-fried croutons
Grapes	Glass of dry sherry
Salt and pepper	
Powdered bay leaf or	
¼ bay leaf	

To each quail allow 6 grapes skinned, pipped and cut in halves. Stuff the birds with these. Mix the butter to a paste with a little salt, pepper, and a touch of powdered bay leaf (or ¼ of a whole bay leaf) and rosemary. Rub this mixture all over the birds. Roast quickly at gas mark 8, 450°F (230°C) for 15–20 minutes. Remove birds to warm serving dish, standing each on a tiny butter-fried croûton. Pour a glass of dry sherry into the roasting tin, swirl this round and reduce to a syrupy consistency. Pour a dribble over each bird. Add extra grapes as garnish if liked.

Elegant fish and chips

Serves 4 or 5

There is only one way to improve on good northern fish and chips, eaten straight out of the paper, crisp and hot, and that is to borrow an idea from the French (did you ever think I would admit to such a thing?). Fish cooked *à l'orly* or in a crisp batter is marinated first in a little oil and lemon juice before frying.

This is ideal when batter-frying fillets of whiting or even perch as it gives an added dimension to things and an up-market slant in that the French make a slightly lighter batter. My batter recipe is a cross between the two countries and ideal for use in either one of them.

Batter

4 oz white flour	1 egg yolk
4 tbsp milk	4 tbsp beer
½ tsp salt	2 egg whites

Sieve the flour and salt into a mixing bowl, make a well, mix beer and yolk together and pour into the well. Gradually incorporate the flour adding enough milk to form a smooth batter.

Leave the batter to rest for half-an-hour. Just before using thoroughly fold in the stiffly-beaten egg whites.

To fry the fish

2 lb firm-fleshed fish fillets such as haddock, cod, plaice, sole, flounder, etc., skinned, rinsed and patted dry and cut into even-sized pieces approximately 2 × 4 inches.

Marinade (optional)

3 tbsp olive oil	¼ tsp finely grated lemon rind
2 tbsp lemon juice	¼ tsp crushed garlic (optional)
1 tbsp freshly chopped parsley	Salt and milled pepper

Mix all the ingredients together. Put in the fish pieces and leave to marinate for ½ hour, turning them from time to time.

Drop 3 or 4 pieces of marinated fish into the prepared batter making sure each piece is well coated before lowering them gently into hot fat or oil at 375°F (190°C). Fry for 4 to 5 minutes depending on the size and thickness of the piece and turning them with a slotted spoon a couple of times.

When cooked, drain the pieces on a wire rack or crumpled kitchen paper. Serve on a dish paper on a heated platter, with lemon wedges and Tartare sauce.

Crisp Chips
2 lb potatoes, peeled and cut   Fat or oil for deep frying
   into even-sized chips.

Pat the chips dry in a kitchen towel. For the first frying immerse the chips in a basket in a deep fryer with the fat or oil heated to 360°F (180°C).

When the chips are cooked through (soft) but still pale, lift the basket out. Drain the chips. (This is known as blanching.) Re-heat the fat to 400°F (200°C). Plunge the chips into the smoking fat for a minute or until crisp and golden brown. Shake the basket, before tipping the chips on to crumpled paper. Salt them lightly before serving.

Fry the chips at both stages in 3 or 4 batches (or about ½ lb at a time). If too many are fried at once the temperature of the oil and fat will be reduced and the chips will be soggy. If you have to keep chips waiting, leave the oven door open so that they stay crisp.

Crunchy-topped fish pie

Serves 4

2 lb cod or haddock fillet   4 oz peeled prawns
1 pint hot Rich white sauce   2 hard-boiled eggs
   (page 117)   1 tbsp chives and/or parsley

Topping
2 oz white breadcrumbs   Mashed potatoes *see* Method
2 oz butter

Make up the Rich white sauce. Put the poached, skinned and flaked fish into a buttered ovenproof dish. Add the prawns, chopped hard-boiled eggs and finely chopped chives to the hot sauce and pour over the fish.

Fry the breadcrumbs in the butter until buttery crisp. Whip the potatoes with a goodly knob of butter and a big spoonful of cream (I use four jacket-baked potatoes scooped out, which are much tastier than boiled potatoes).

Fork a cushion of potatoes over the coated fish, sprinkle with the breadcrumbs and heat the pie through in the oven at gas mark 6, 400°F (200°C) until bubbling hot.

Hot fish mousse

Serves 6

1½ lb cod fillets, skinned	¾ pint double cream
6 egg whites	2 tsp salt
6 oz fresh or frozen cranberries (not tinned)	¼ tsp ground mace

Sauce

2 oz butter	6 oz Ocean Spray jellied cranberry sauce
Juice of 1 lemon	

Mince the fish several times through finest blade of a mincer or run through food processor. Gradually beat in egg whites. Chill for 30 minutes. Gradually beat in cream. Mix in cranberries, salt and mace.

Butter a mould and fill with fish mixture. Cover with buttered foil. Place mould into a pan of hot water coming halfway up the sides. Bake in preheated oven, gas mark 3, 325°F (170°C), for 1 hour or until firm to the touch.

Remove from oven and allow to stand for 15 minutes. Loosen edges and unmould on to serving platter. Cut into slices and serve warm topped with cranberry sauce.

To prepare sauce, heat butter with cranberry sauce and lemon juice until bubbly and smooth: press through a fine sieve, season and re-heat.

Braised farm trout with artichokes
Serves 4

4 10 oz trout
2 oz seasoned flour
2 oz butter
1 small onion, finely sliced
3 small tomatoes, skinned,
  seeded and chopped

½ pint medium dry white wine
Piece of stock cube
¼ pint double cream
½ tsp grated orange zest
¼ tsp ground nutmeg

Garnish
1 8 oz tin artichoke hearts,
  drained and quartered

Gut, clean and wash the fish: cut off heads and tails, pat dry on kitchen paper towels. Dredge lightly in seasoned flour, shaking off surplus flour.

Melt butter in large heavy-bottomed frying pan until foaming. Quickly brown the trout on each side, remove to a plate. Over a gentle heat fry the onion until golden and soft. Add the tomatoes and wine, crumble in the bit of stock cube, simmer for a minute.

Return the trout to the pan, cover with a lid or foil. Simmer or poach the fish for 2 to 3 minutes on each side. Remove to a warm serving dish (remove skin if preferred). Add the nutmeg and orange to the pan. Reduce the pan liquids to about a quarter of a pint by boiling rapidly. Add the cream and allow to boil for a minute. Strain the sauce over the waiting fish. Heat the artichoke hearts in an ounce of butter, and arrange round the fish.

Cold poached trout with orange and tarragon
Serves 4

4 trout weighing about 8 to
  10 oz each
¼ pint oil for frying

2 oz plain white flour for
  dredging
Salt and freshly milled pepper

For the marinade
1 tbsp good olive oil
1 small onion, sliced
½ pint dry white vermouth
½ pint carton orange juice

The finely grated zest of
  1 orange
Salt and freshly milled pepper

For the garnish

2 oranges, peeled and
    segmented or cut into slices

1 tbsp chopped fresh tarragon,
    or parsley

Clean and decapitate the trout, cut off the fins and tail. In a frying pan large enough to contain the fish, heat the oil until lightly smoking. Dip each fish in seasoned flour and fry gently for 3 minutes on each side. Remove them to a shallow (1½ inch deep) serving dish. Make 2 or 3 incisions in each fish.

In a non-aluminium pan, bring all the ingredients for the marinade to the boil. Lower the heat and simmer for 15 minutes.

Pour the hot marinade over the waiting trout. Leave to cool completely. Sprinkle over the tarragon or parsley. Cover with plastic film and refrigerate for 4 to 5 hours or overnight. Serve, topped with orange segments. Some people do not enjoy fish skin, in which case remove the skin when the fish is cool before covering with marinade and do not make the incisions.

Trout with oranges, almonds and capers

Serves 4

Trout is always a popular fish and relatively economical. Try this combination of garnishes next time you have some fresh trout from one of our beautiful rivers.

4 trout (approx 8 oz each)
Seasoned flour

Good oil and butter

Garnish

2 oranges
2 oz sweet flaked almonds
1 tbsp large juicy capers

Salt and pepper
Orange juice

As butter burns readily it is a good idea to use a mixture of oil and butter for frying. Dredge each fish in seasoned flour and fry on both sides until cooked. About 4 minutes a side will suffice, but a good test is to press the flesh with the tip of your finger and if it 'gives' readily then they are cooked.

Remove the fish to a warm serving dish whilst you finish off the garnish. If the fats in which you have fried the fish are too dark then discard these and restart with a good 2 oz of butter. Lightly brown the almonds in this, adding a little orange juice to arrest the frying process when they are ready, as almonds can burn with residual heat. Have the oranges 'knife-peeled' and segmented. Warm these through with the browned almonds, strew in the capers, season and pour the whole lot over the waiting fish . . . delicious!

Fillet of sole with cranberries and leeks

Serves 4

8 fillets of Dover sole
8 leeks, white part only, cut
   into julienne strips
Salt and pepper
¼ pint dry white wine
¼ pint water

6 oz Ocean Spray cranberries
½ tsp sugar
½ pint double cream
Snipped chives

Season sole and leeks with salt and pepper. Poach sole and leeks in a mixture of wine and water for 6 minutes. Remove sole and leeks to a serving platter and keep warm. They should not be overcooked. Retain liquid.

Add cranberries and sugar and boil until liquid is reduced to half its original volume. Add cream and continue boiling until sauce is slightly thickened. Season to taste with salt and pepper. Spoon sauce over sole and leeks.

Serve sprinkled with chopped chives. It can be served garnished with 16 to 20 melon balls or cubes which have been sautéed with 2 tablespoons butter and 1 tablespoon raspberry *or* red wine vinegar until hot and glazed.

Fillet of plaice caprice

Serves 4

4 large plaice fillets, skinned
Seasoned flour
2 oz good butter for frying
2 bananas, cut in half
   lengthways

Salt and pepper
Lemon juice
2 tbsp fruit chutney, pressed
   through a fine sieve and
   heated in a small pan

Dip each fillet in seasoned flour and shake away any surplus. Melt the butter evenly in a large frying pan, twisting and turning the pan to ensure this. When it is 'quiet' and giving off an almondy smell, gently lower in the fillets one at a time, keeping the butter to temperature. Lightly salt and pepper.

Fry the fillets quickly on each side (1½ to 2 minutes each way will suffice). Remove them to a warm serving platter. Fry the bananas in the same way, until they are golden brown but not broken up. Arrange a fried banana half atop each fillet. Squeeze about a dessertspoon of lemon juice into the pan, swirl this round and strain on to the fillets. Dribble a spoonful of sieved chutney down the side of each banana.

Poached plaice with oranges and anchovy

Serves 4

4 large fillets of plaice	1 tbsp chives, chopped
Dry white wine (or cider) to cover	½ oz butter
	Salt and milled white pepper

Sauce

¼ pint single cream	1 egg yolk
¼ tsp arrowroot	

Garnish

1 orange, segmented	1 tbsp capers
8 anchovy fillets	Chopped parsley

Butter the bottom of a shallow pan. Season the fillets and sprinkle with the chopped chives: fold or roll them.

Put in the pan and cover with wine or cider, then with a circle of buttered greaseproof paper and a lid. Bring to the boil, then simmer for 5 minutes. Remove fillets to a warm serving dish. Reduce the wine liquid to ¼ pint. Mix arrowroot, cream and egg yolk to a smooth consistency. Whisk the hot liquor into this, reheat just to boiling point (but do not allow to actually boil). Check the seasoning. Strain sauce over waiting fillets.

Garnish with a cross of anchovy fillets and two orange segments for each fillet. Sprinkle with capers and parsley.

Filets de sole au vin rouge (Fillets of sole in red wine)

Serves 4

8 fillets of Dover Sole, skinned	*Beurre-manié* (page 13)
Red Burgundy	2 oz French butter cut into
2 oz field mushrooms	half inch cubes, softened at
1 oz onions	room temperature
½ chicken stock cube	Salt and pepper

Select a shallow pan (a frying pan would do) large enough to contain the fillets, folded once, in one layer. Butter the pan lightly, cut a circle of greaseproof paper to fit the surface of the pan and butter this too.

Gently bat the fillets with a wetted rolling pin (wetting prevents the flesh from dragging and tearing; gentle batting breaks down the tissue enough to prevent the fillets from curling up). Season each fillet lightly with salt and pepper and fold in half. Finely chop the mushrooms and onion and sprinkle evenly over the base of the pan. Arrange the fillets on top in one layer.

Pour over enough red wine to just cover. Put the buttered paper circle on top then put on a lid. Bring the contents to boiling point, reduce the heat and simmer the fish for 6 to 7 minutes.

Remove the paper (which will have collected any scum precipitated). Remove the fillets to a warm serving dish (cover with a damp clean cloth to prevent them drying out) and keep warm. Add the ½ stock cube to the pan.

Boil the contents of the pan rapidly until the liquid is reduced by half. Strain into a small pan. Whisk in *tiny* bits of *beurre-manié* until the sauce is smooth and glossy. Allow the liquid to boil and thicken between each addition. The consistency should be that of single cream. (The colour will be approximately like blackcurrant juice and cream.)

Just before serving, stand the dish containing the cooked fillets near where you are working at the side of the stove. Bring the sauce to the boil. Remove from the heat. Using a small balloon whisk, beat in the softened bits of butter.

The sauce will increase in volume and become unctuous. *Do not return to the heat.* Pour over the fish and serve immediately.

You have successfully 'mounted' a sauce. This sauce will not re-heat as the emulsion will break down but is delicious served cold.

Pan-baked mackerel with lemon, rosemary and garlic

Serves 4

4 mackerel weighing about 10 to 12 oz each
4 tbsp olive oil (or mixture of olive and vegetable oil)
2 oz butter
4 cloves garlic, peeled and crushed

1 small sprig fresh rosemary or ¼ tsp dried ground rosemary per fish
Juice of half a large lemon
Salt and freshly milled pepper
Extra lemon wedges

Clean and decapitate the mackerel, cut off the fins and tail, wash well under running water. Drain and pat dry with paper towels. Put a small sprig or ¼ tsp of dried rosemary into each cavity.

In a large non-stick frying pan, heat the oil and butter until foaming. Add the garlic and fry for a minute or so. Add the mackerel, add more rosemary. Brown the fish on both sides over a good heat, seasoning on both sides. Pour over the lemon juice, lower the heat, cover with a lid and simmer the fish gently for 15 minutes or until the fish 'gives' in the thickest part when pressed with the forefinger.

Remove the fish to warm dinner plates. Spoon a little of the pan juices over each fish and serve piping hot with extra lemon wedges.

Salmon and egg pie

Serves 4 to 5 as a main course, 6 to 8 as a starter

Shortcrust pastry
6 oz plain white flour
Water to mix
2 oz butter

2 oz lard
Salt

Salmon and egg filling
1 lb flaked cooked fish, salmon, tuna, haddock or tinned salmon
3 hard-boiled eggs, roughly chopped

2 tbsp chopped parsley, fresh basil or tarragon or all three mixed
Tinned juice or poaching stock

Choux pastry topping

3 oz good butter	4 small eggs, well beaten
8 fl oz water	4 oz Dutch or other melting
4 oz plain strong white flour	cheese, cut into ¼ inch dice
½ tsp salt	

Sauce

1 oz flour	¾ pint of milk infused with
2 oz butter	onion, bay leaf and thyme

Make up shortcrust pastry in the usual way. Line a 10 inch, 2 inch deep, loose bottomed pie tin with the pastry. Bake blind at gas mark 7, 425°F (220°C) for 20 minutes.

To make the filling

Mix fish, chopped eggs and herbs in a large bowl. Include the juice from tinned fish or a little stock if you have poached your own to help bind together.

To make the sauce

Infuse the milk with the onion, bay leaf and thyme over a low heat for 30 minutes. Melt the butter, stir in the flour and add the milk gradually, after straining it. Bring to boil, stirring to thicken.

To make the choux pastry

Sieve the flour and salt on to a paper. Melt the butter with water in a pan and tip the flour in at one fell swoop. Beat well with a wooden spatula until the mixture leaves the sides of the pan clean. Gradually beat in the eggs until the pastry is glossy, and add the diced cheese.

Carefully fold the *hot* sauce into the filling and spoon the mixture into the pastry shell. Top with choux pastry and bake at gas mark 7, 425°F (220°C) for 40–45 minutes or until puffed up and cooked through.

Kedgeree

Serves 5 to 6

I fear tempers would fly and argument ensue if one was to attempt to define just what a true Kedgeree is.

That it came to us from India, when that great country was part of our Empire, cannot be denied; but what happened to it after its arrival is anyone's guess.

What do persist through the many versions of this dish are the two basic ingredients – fish and rice. Many say that it can only be made with smoked haddock; others say that eggs are essential. I have even heard it said that the Irish thought the whole thing up! Curry appears in some recipes, and this would seem logical in the light of its place of origin. There are those who like it very dry, but I like mine made with salmon (or smoked haddock), eggs, mushrooms, and with a very creamy sauce. I have also moved its time of appearance from the breakfast table to the lunch table, unless I indulge in that Americanisation 'brunch' where it fits perfectly.

12 oz tin middle-cut salmon (or ¾ lb piece cooked fresh salmon or smoked haddock)	Tip of tsp curry powder
	½ stock cube
	Juice of half a lemon
1 small onion	4 hard-boiled eggs
1 pint milk	6 oz rice
1 oz plain flour	Fresh parsley, chopped
2 oz butter	Salt and freshly ground pepper
4 oz button mushrooms	¼ pint single cream (optional – *see* Method)

Boil the eggs for no more than 10 minutes, assuming that they were cold to start with. They should still have a ¼ inch of soft centre. Run them under cold water until they are quite cold and then shell them. Cut them into quarters and then into eighths. Cover with plastic film until you require them.

Cook the rice in plenty of boiling light-salted water for 17 minutes exactly, then run it under the cold tap and wash off the starch. Leave to drain in a sieve or colander.

Finely slice the onion and mushrooms. Melt the butter in a pan which will be large enough to contain all the ingredients. Add the sliced onions and fry until golden brown, then add the mushrooms and fry for a few seconds before stirring in the flour.

Add the touch of curry powder and the piece of stock cube.

Gradually work in the cold milk a little at a time until you have a smooth sauce and simmer for 5 minutes, stirring to ensure that it doesn't stick or burn.

If using tinned salmon, pour the juices from the tin into the sauce. Correct the seasoning and add lemon juice to acidulate lightly. Skin and flake the fish and fold into the sauce, then fold in the cooked rice and gently allow this to heat through, stirring with a 'folding' action as you do so, so that you do not break up the fish too much.

Finally, just before you are ready to serve the kedgeree, carefully fold in the eggs. Pour the kedgeree into a heated dish, sprinkle with parsley and serve. If the finished dish is too solid for you, add a ¼ pint of single cream brought to the boil. I sometimes serve the rice separately, as it is possible to make it look more attractive this way, particularly if you mould the rice in a buttered ring-mould first, then fill the centre with the salmon (or haddock), eggs and mushrooms in their creamy sauce.

Salmon mousse

Serves 8

1½ lb middle-cut Scotch
  salmon
1 small onion
1 carrot
1 sprig dill weed or parsley
Water
Salt and peppercorns

½ pint Basic mayonnaise
  (see page 129)
½ pint double cream
Juice of ½ a lemon
Salt and freshly ground
  white pepper

Aspic (*see* Method)
Fish stock

1 oz gelatine

Garnish
Commercial aspic
Dry white wine

Tomato
Cucumber

Select a pan just large enough to hold the piece of salmon. For a piece as small as this there is little purpose in using a fish-kettle.

Wash and scale the fish and leave it ready to poach. Fill the pan with enough water to just cover the fish. (Stand a small oiled plate on the bottom of the pan to prevent the skin from sticking.)

Peel the onion and the carrot and cut them into quarters. Add these to the water, together with the dill or parsley and a little salt. Bring the liquid to the boil and simmer for 10 minutes before lowering in the piece of salmon.

Poach the salmon for 20 minutes only, and leave it to cool in the poaching liquor. Remember that to poach means to cook so slowly that the water is only just moving.

When the fish is cool, lift out the salmon and skin it. Take away the dark 'band' down the spine, using a teaspoon to help you. Carefully remove every bone and then pound the fish flesh in a heavy basin (or in a mortar).

Put this pounded fish on one side whilst you make the Basic mayonnaise and aspic.

To make the aspic, first measure half a pint of fish stock; pour through a strainer into a pan and bring to the boil. Add the gelatine and dissolve (this is double the usual amount of gelatine, as the aspic has to 'support' quite a lot of ingredients). Pour into a bowl.

Arrange the bowl in a sink of running cold water, making sure that there is no chance of any of the water getting into the aspic! Stir from time to time to ensure even cooling; don't let it set.

Whip the cream until it just starts to ribbon but is not stiff.

Put the salmon into a large bowl and season with a little more salt, a modicum of freshly ground white pepper and a little lemon juice.

Beat in the mayonnaise and add more seasoning if you feel it necessary. Pour in the cold, but not set, aspic and incorporate thoroughly. Fold in the half-whipped cream carefully but thoroughly.

Pour the mixture into a mould or soufflé dish – if you intend to unmould the mousse, the container should be lightly oiled and a circle of greaseproof paper fitted in the bottom. It is probably much simpler, however, to leave the mousse in its dish. Cover with foil, and put into the refrigerator to set.

If serving mousse in its dish make up ½ pint of commercial aspic jelly with the normal amount of crystals asked for on the packet but using half dry white wine and half water.

Let the jelly cool, but not set, then run a thin layer over the top of the mousse and return it to the refrigerator to give the jelly time to set.

Stir the remaining aspic with a warm spoon to ensure that it doesn't suddenly set.

Decorate the mousse as you will. You can decorate the top

quite professionally with sections of egg-white, blanched tarragon leaves or sprays of dill, quarters of unpeeled cucumber, strips of skinned and deseeded tomato, olive rings, etc. Then very carefully float a little more jelly on the top to 'fix' the decoration. Put this again in the refrigerator. Finally, float the rest of aspic on to the top. If you follow this method of decorating, the pieces will not float away and leave you frustrated!

Serve the mousse with Sauce mousseline (page 124) seasoned to taste with lemon juice.

Smoked haddock mousse

Serves 6

1 lb smoked haddock (weighed, skinned and boned)	Parsley stalks
	½ pint bland mayonnaise (see page 129)
Lemon juice	½ pint double cream
1 bay leaf	Salt and freshly milled white pepper
½ onion	

Aspic jelly
½ pint fish liquor   1 oz gelatine

Garnish
¾ pint commercial aspic   Cucumber segments
Tomato quarters

Poach the haddock in slightly salted water acidulated with a little lemon juice and flavoured with a few parsley stalks, a bay leaf and a piece of onion. Drain (retaining the liquor). Remove any skin and bone.

For the aspic jelly strain ½ pint of the cooking liquor and dissolve the gelatine in this. Allow to cool. Whip the cream until it 'ribbons' (leaving a definite trail but does not quite stand in peaks).

Put flaked haddock and aspic into blender and blend until quite fine. Season well at this stage. Beat in the mayonnaise, then fold in the cream. Pour into a soufflé dish or glass bowl. Chill until set (4 hours in average refrigerator).

Make up the commercial aspic as instructed on packet. To coat the mousse float an ⅛ inch layer of cool aspic jelly on top. Return bowl to refrigerator to set. Next arrange on top any garnish you choose, pouring just a dribble of aspic over this to 'fix it'. Set again. Now finish with a top layer of aspic.

Decorate at will and serve, accompanied by a boat of lemon-flavoured creamy mayonnaise.

Finnan haddock with parsley sauce
Serves 6

This gets one away from the piece of smoked haddock afloat in a pint of milk. It retains its delicious flavour, and combines it successfully with a version of one of England's most popular sauces. An old aunt of mine always served her haddocks this way, and for years I thought she was a competent 'continental' cook! She showed me how to make it when I was fourteen. The traditional poached egg can crown the finished dish.

3 lb smoked haddock
2 pints cold water
Squeeze of lemon

1 sprig parsley
Salt and freshly ground white
    pepper

Parsley Sauce
½ pint poaching liquid
½ pint single cream
3 oz butter
Pinch of castor sugar
1 oz plain flour

2 heaped tbsp fresh, finely
    chopped parsley
A little lemon juice
Salt and freshly ground white
    pepper

Wash the fish: cut into serving pieces.

Lightly oil the bottom of a shallow pan and put in the pieces of fish; cover with the water, season lightly, add sprig of parsley and squeeze of lemon juice, then cover with a circle of oiled paper to fit the surface. Put a lid on the pan and poach slowly (rapid boiling breaks up the flesh), until the fish is just cooked – about 10 minutes.

Remove the fish, taking out any bones and skin; arrange in a warm serving dish, cover with a damp cloth or wetted paper *and* a lid, and put to keep warm. Reduce the cooking liquor down to half a pint by boiling rapidly.

Melt the butter in a small pan, stir in the flour, strain the fish stock on to this and whisk the sauce until it is smooth. Add the cream and cook for 5 minutes over a very low heat, stirring all the time. Check the seasoning – there will probably be enough salt.

Add a little lemon juice and a pinch of sugar. Stir in the abundance of parsley (I sometimes add a few chopped chives), pour over the waiting fish and serve immediately.

This rich, bright green parsley sauce is a worthy addition to any repertoire. The same technique can be used for any fish which you want to serve in this way. It is always well to keep a little stock back, just in case the flour you are using is 'stronger' than usual and you wish to thin the sauce down a little.

Smoked haddock, bacon and mushroom fishcakes

Serves 4

12 oz flaked, cooked smoked
    haddock (weighed after
    skinning and boning)
4 rashers bacon
2 oz onion, finely chopped
¼ tsp ground nutmeg
Flour
Beaten egg
Fresh white breadcrumbs

4 oz mushrooms, finely
    chopped
1 small (2 to 3 servings) sachet
    of instant potato
    reconstituted
1 beaten egg
Salt and pepper
Butter

Dice the bacon, fry until crisp, remove from pan with a draining spoon.

Add a knob of butter to the pan. Fry onion in the pan fats until golden-brown and soft. Fry the mushrooms for a minute or so. Mix the mushrooms, onions and bacon with the flaked fish, and reconstituted potato.

Season lightly (take care with the salt as the smoked haddock may be salty enough). Add nutmeg. Bind with the beaten egg. Leave to chill and firm up. Press out into a 1 inch thick mass on a floured worktop. Cut into 3 inch rounds with a plain scone cutter. Coat each round in flour, beaten egg and breadcrumbs. Fry in hot fat or oil until golden-brown, allowing 2 to 3 minutes on each side. Makes approximately 8 cakes.

Tandoori fish with mushroom kebabs

Serves 4

5 fl oz natural yoghurt	3 tsp paprika pepper
1 medium onion, finely chopped	2 tsp lemon juice
	3 tsp vinegar
2 dashes Tabasco sauce	1 tbsp nut or olive oil
1 tbsp Soy sauce	½ tsp ground ginger
2 tbsp curry powder	½ tsp salt
4 thick pieces haddock or cod	8 oz button mushrooms

Mix all the ingredients together except fish and mushrooms. Remove any apparent bones from fish. Make 2 or 3 incisions in each piece. Marinate fish and mushrooms in the yoghurt mixture for at least four hours, covered, in the refrigerator. Thread mushrooms on to skewers, and place fish on the grilling rack.

Brush mushrooms with remaining yoghurt mixture. Cook the fish under the hot grill for about 5 minutes on each side, depending on thickness, until cooked. During the final 5 minutes grill the mushroom kebabs and turn them frequently. Garnish with lemon wedges.

Kippers with marmalade

This way of doing kippers does not work so well for those who insist on hanging their kippers upside down in a jug of water! Or who poach or boil them thus ridding them of their natural juicy succulence.

Kippers	Seville marmalade
Butter	

Grill the kippers with a knob of butter. Add a dribble of sieved hot Seville marmalade down the spine of each just before serving.

Devilled whitebait

Allow 6 to 8 oz of whitebait per serving. Wash them well under cold running water and pat them dry with kitchen paper towels.

Dip them in milk, drain them, then dredge them well in white flour lightly seasoned with salt and pepper.

Deep fry the whitebait in batches in lightly smoking oil. They will only take a couple of minutes but should be crisp and golden-brown when cooked. If they are limp or soggy allow the oil in the fryer to get back to temperature then plunge them in again to crispen. (If they are soggy this will be for one of two reasons. The fat or oil was not to temperature, or too many whitebait were put into the pan, thus lowering the temperature too much.) Shake and drain them on crumpled paper (newspaper will do!).

Dredge them lightly with cayenne pepper and a smidge more salt.

Serve with a goodly piece of lemon or lime and thinly cut brown bread and butter.

Crispy tuna pie
Serves 4

7 oz can tuna	½ pint milk
½ oz butter	Salt and pepper
¾ oz cornflour	4 hard-boiled eggs

Topping

3 oz plain flour	Small packet potato crisps,
1½ oz butter	crushed
2 oz cheddar cheese, grated	Salt, pepper and a little mace

Drain 2 tablespoons of oil from canned tuna into a saucepan, and add the butter to it. Melt over low heat, then add cornflour and mix thoroughly.

Remove from heat, and add milk gradually while stirring. Return to medium heat and bring to boil while stirring. Add seasoning. Add tuna, breaking it up a little.

Cut eggs into quarters and arrange in a 2 pint ovenproof dish. Pour mixture on top. For topping rub butter into flour. Mix in cheese, crisps and seasoning, not too much salt, then scatter crumble evenly over the mixture. Bake in oven gas mark 5, 375°F (190°C), for 25 to 30 minutes.

Sauce and fish combine conveniently to make a delicious contrast with the crumble topping. Garnish with fresh tomato slices. For more sophisticated tastes add 1 teaspoon dried mixed herbs to the crumble mixture.

Insalata di mare (Mixed seafood salad)
Serves 8

Sambuca is my favourite London Italian restaurant. Here is Signor Sandros' recipe for their *Insalata di mare* – Mixed seafood salad.

6 medium sized squids
6 scallops
½ lb jumbo scampi, peeled
2 pints fresh mussels, cleaned
½ lb peeled prawns

½ lb prawns in their shells
½ pint fresh clams, cleaned
 (or small tin if unavailable)
½ lemon
Salt

Garnish
1 green pepper
1 red pepper
8 large gherkins
1 tbsp capers
8 whole red chillies
Juice of 4 lemons

1 tsp chopped oregano
 or parsley
¾ pint olive oil
1 clove garlic, crushed
Salt and ground black pepper

Detach the tentacles of the squids from the bodies. Wash and clean the fish carefully. Boil the body for 20 minutes, and the tentacles for 30 minutes longer in salted water with ½ lemon.

When cooked slice the fish into rings; and split the tentacles. Re-wash the fish and dry. Split the scallops into two parts and put in a pan with the peeled scampi. Bring to the boil and allow to cool in the liquor.

Immerse the mussels in boiling water and cover, add a little salt. As soon as mussels open remove at once from heat and allow to cool. Separate the mussels from the shells. Cook clams in the same way as mussels, but leave in their shells.

Slice the peppers and gherkins into thin strips. Mix all the fish, except the prawns in shells in a large bowl with the oil and lemon juice, and add salt and pepper and the rest of the garnish ingredients. Leave the chillies whole. Mix well and taste. Cover with plastic film and chill.

If the dressing is not sharp enough, add more lemon. Allow preparation to marinate for a few hours, remixing before serving. Arrange the prawns in their shells around the serving dish with wedges of lemon.

Mini brochettes of scallop, bacon and pear
Serves 4

4 fat scallops
1 large ripe but firm pear
4 rashers of streaky bacon

Juice of half a large lemon
1 tbsp olive oil
Salt and pepper

Cut each scallop into 6 to 8 pieces. Peel and core the pear, cut into pieces the same size as the scallops. Toss both in lemon juice and oil. Season lightly. Cut the bacon into small pieces. Skewer on to slim sticks, grill under a spanking hot grill for 4 to 5 minutes, turning them to ensure even grilling. Serve with savoury rice. Makes 8.

Langoustines flamed in whisky

I cannot imagine you will *want* to cook these live, but if you *can* buy live langoustines then I recommend you do this. De-frosted Mediterranean prawns will do equally well, or crayfish tails or prawns. Allow 5 to 6 fish per serving.

You will need butter for frying, a little crushed garlic, whisky for blazing.
Salt and pepper should be put on by individual guests.

Just how many you do at once will depend on the size of your frying or sauté pan. Let's assume your pan holds 8 to 10 fish.
Melt 2 oz of butter to foaming point. Add 1 clove of garlic crushed. Stir this round. Add the fish. Turn and stir them until hot right through (or cooked if raw about 5 to 6 minutes).
When all is hot and sizzling, pour in 2 fl oz of whisky. Lean away from the pan, and tip it to the flame or ignite with a match. The flame should shoot heavenwards!
Pass the allotted number to each guest, basted with the pan juices, and with a lemon wedge, large napkin and finger bowl (or a hot steaming scented towel). Surprisingly you don't have to travel on Japanese airlines to have these! Just spray guest towels (terry-towelling variety) with your favourite after-shave (sorry, cologne, scent or rose-flower water). Put them into an ordinary domestic steamer for 20 minutes. Use a pair of kitchen tongs to lift them out of the steamer, and parcel them in a large towel, arranged on a small tray to transport them to the table. It's a

marvellous touch, and the first time you do this in Penrith your success as a hostess will be ensured for life. There is little point in attempting to eat these fish in any other way but with the fingers.

Vegetables

Potatoes with cream and coarse nutmeg

2 lb even-sized new potatoes
¼ pint double cream

1 level tsp coarsely ground
  nutmeg

Wash the potatoes well leaving their skins on. Boil in lightly salted water until just cooked. Drain and dry over a low heat. Pour over the cream and sprinkle on the nutmeg, toss the potatoes round until they are evenly coated. Serve very hot.

Potato latkes

Yields 24 to 30

5 large potatoes to yield 1½ lb
  of grated potato when
  peeled
3 oz plain white flour
1 tsp salt
2 eggs, beaten
1 large onion, grated

¼ pint single cream
Milled pepper to taste
¼ tsp bicarbonate of soda
Garlic
Oil for frying

Grate the potatoes on the coarse side of a grater or in a food processor.

Drop them as you go along into a large bowl of cold water, into which you have put the bicarbonate. This helps keep them a good colour.

Leave them to soak for an hour. Drain well, and pat excess moisture away. Mix with the flour, onion, garlic, beaten eggs and cream. Season well.

Heat ¼ inch of oil in a heavy-bottomed frying pan, until lightly smoking. Drop teaspoons of the mixture into the oil and fry on both sides until cooked and golden-brown.

Drain on a crumpled kitchen paper.

Serve hot.

Brandied cheese potatoes

Once in a while a cook will come up with a new idea which really is stunning and yet not costly. I think I have such a notion for you. These potatoes, again readily prepared for they can be done a day in advance, are ideal for serving with any grilled meat. They would also make a good supper dish.

4 medium-sized waxy potatoes baked in their jackets	2 tbsp brandy
2 oz butter	3 oz grated Dutch cheese
1 good tbsp bland mayonnaise	Salt and a little milled pepper

Cut a lid from each potato, scoop out the flesh and mash with the remaining ingredients. Don't be tempted to do this in a food processor or the potato mixture will be glutinous. The texture should be somewhat rough hewn.

Put the mixture back into the potato shells, dredge with further cheese if desired and reheat the potatoes at gas mark 7, 425°F (220°C) or until hot and golden brown.

Pyt i panna (Bacon and potato fry-up)

Serves 4 or 5

The ingredients in this Scandinavian speciality are cooked separately, unlike most hashed dishes.

2 large onions, cut into small dice	1 fried egg or 1 egg yolk per serving
1 lb bacon, cut into small dice	Salt and milled pepper if needed
6 medium waxy potatoes, cut into small dice	Any extra bits of cold meat cut into small dice (optional)
1 tbsp chopped chives and/or parsley	Oil for frying

Fry the bacon until crisp. Remove with a slotted spoon and set aside. Fry the onions in the bacon fat, adding a little butter if necessary. When they are a good brown remove with a slotted spoon and set aside.

Strain the fat into a second, or clean, frying pan, add the oil and when it is smoking add the potatoes, patted dry with a kitchen paper towel.

Fry them over a good heat until they too are brown and cooked through (about 15–20 minutes). Discard any surplus oil. Add bacon and onions, and make thoroughly hot. Season if necessary.

Divide into serving portions on hot dinner plates. Sprinkle with the herbs, top with a fried egg or sit an egg yolk in its shell on top. Serve whilst piping hot.

If any left-over meat is used, this is added to the potatoes with the bacon and onions.

Carrot purée

The purée can be made up to the day before.

3 lbs carrots, cleaned, peeled and cut into pieces
Chicken stock (use a stock cube)

2 oz butter
1 level tsp castor sugar
1 level tsp grated orange zest
1 level tsp ground mace

Cook the carrots in enough well-seasoned chicken stock to cover them, until quite tender. Drain well (retaining the liquid for a soup on some other occasion). Dry over a low heat.

Purée in the blender adding the butter, sugar, zest and mace and more salt if necessary.

To serve Heat ⅛ pint of thick cream in a non-stick pan. Add the purée gradually, stirring over a low heat until it is piping hot.

Beetroots in orange sauce

Select young even-sized beets and cook them in the usual way ensuring that all the soil has been washed off before boiling.

Stock cube
½ pint water
1 small onion, finely sliced
1 dsp tomato purée
1 small clove garlic, crushed
¼ tsp curry powder

Juice of 2 oranges
Grated rind of 1 orange
1 oz butter
1 oz flour
Salt and pepper

Melt the butter in a saucepan, add the onion and fry until golden brown. Stir in the flour, add ½ pint stock (stock cube should be made up at double strength) and orange juice, bring to the boil; add the purée, garlic, curry powder, orange rind and lightly season. Simmer for 10 minutes; strain and serve poured over the sliced beetroots.

Oignons Monégasques (Sweet and sour onions)

1 lb tiny pickling onions
4 fl oz red wine vinegar
6 fl oz water
4 fl oz olive oil
3 oz tomato purée
2 bay leaves
½ tsp dried thyme

Parsley stalks (optional)
6 oz seedless raisins (or sultanas)
1 oz brown sugar
Salt
Freshly milled pepper

Peel all the onions and put into a pan together with all the other ingredients. Cover with a lid, bring to the boil and simmer for 15 to 20 minutes when the onions will be tender but not collapsed. If the sauce isn't thick enough remove the onions with a draining spoon and boil the sauce rapidly until it is viscous. Remove bay leaves and parsley stalks. Cool before chilling.

Serve in individual ramekins or glasses with a small wedge of lemon and French bread and butter. If, in the summer months, you have some fresh basil, a little of this chopped and sprinkled over is good.

Cauliflower with egg and shrimp sauce

1 medium cauliflower
A little lemon juice
Salt

Sauce
4 oz frozen shrimps (or prawns) in their shells
2 eggs
1½ oz butter
¾ oz flour
Tip of a tsp paprika

Salt and pepper
½ pint milk
¼ inch piece chicken stock cube
¼ pint single cream

Cook the cauliflower in lemon-acidulated, salted water until cooked but still crisp.

Meanwhile shell the shrimps and hard-boil the eggs. Melt the butter in a small pan, add the empty shrimp shells and stir round for a minute or two. Sprinkle over the flour and the paprika; add the piece of stock cube. Gradually incorporate the milk and simmer the sauce for 10 minutes over a very slow heat. Strain through a fine sieve. Add the cream and adjust the seasoning. Chop the eggs and add to the hot sauce together with the peeled shrimps. Pour over the cauliflower and serve. This makes an excellent starter at dinner parties.

Herbed cabbage

2 lb white cabbage
1 oz butter
1 oz white flour

1 tsp dried thyme
Salt and pepper

Clean the cabbage and shred as fine as possible. Cook very quickly in a pint of boiling water. Strain retaining half a pint of the liquid.

Melt the butter in a small pan, stir in the flour, add the cabbage water and cook until this sauce is smooth. Add the thyme and season lightly, pour the sauce over the cooked cabbage stirring well in.

Mint and pea purée

12 oz frozen peas
2 oz butter
1 level tsp sugar
Salt and pepper

12 mint leaves (or 1 tbsp mint sauce)
¼ tsp finely grated lemon rind

Melt the butter in a pan, add the frozen peas and all the other ingredients; cover with a lid and simmer for no more than 5 minutes; pass the entire contents of the pan through a coarse sieve. Pile into a hot tureen and serve with a dribble of thick cream poured over.

Shaken pease

The name for this dish comes from that of the 18th-century pan used for cooking it – a shaking pan.

12 oz baby frozen peas	1 tbsp thick cream
½ lettuce	1 tsp soft butter
1 clove garlic, finely chopped	1 tsp flour
1 onion	Salt and pepper
1 oz butter	Chopped mint
½ tsp castor sugar	

Melt the ounce of butter, but do not permit to brown. Add the finely sliced onion and garlic, cover the pan with a lid and let these soften without taking on any colour. Add the peas and shake the pan until the juices start to draw (no water is required). Simmer for 2–3 minutes, add the lettuce, very finely shredded, and sugar, season delicately. Simmer for a further 2 minutes. Add the cream. Mix the soft butter and flour to a paste and whisk a little of this in until the whole is just cohered. Stir in freshly chopped mint and serve immediately.

This dish will darken in colour (no detriment) if kept waiting too long.

Asparagus vinaigrette

This can be served as an hors d'oeuvres.

Fresh asparagus	French dressing (*see* page 133)
Salt	

Cook the asparagus for 20 minutes in boiling salted water, then plunge into cold water. Drain well on a clean tea towel as asparagus tends to hold water.

Make up a French dressing adjusting the quantity to your requirements but allowing approximately 1 tablespoonful of dressing per six stalks of asparagus.

Arrange the asparagus in a dish and sprinkle the tips with the dressing.

Courgettes with peas and herbs

4 medium sized (5 inch)
   courgettes
Juice of half a lemon
1 oz butter
8 oz packet frozen *petit pois*
   (defrosted)

1 tbsp freshly chopped herbs
   (basil in the summer or
   oregano) or 1½ tsp dried
   oregano in the winter
1 level tsp castor sugar
Salt and milled pepper

Top, tail and wash the courgettes. Cut into tiny ¼ inch cubes. Toss in the lemon juice to prevent discolouration.

In a shallow, heavy-bottomed pan, melt the butter without browning. Add the peas and courgettes and all the remaining ingredients. Using a slotted spoon, turn and stir gently all the time. Bring them to piping hot. The courgettes should still be somewhat crisp.

Turn into a warm tureen and serve in their own juices.

Courgettes à la Provençale
(Courgettes in tomato sauce with cheese)

2 lb young courgettes
2 lb tomatoes, skinned,
   deseeded and sliced
1 oz butter and 2 tbsp olive oil
2 cloves garlic, finely chopped

Heaped tsp sugar
1 tbsp freshly chopped parsley
6 oz grated Emmental,
   Gruyère or Cheddar cheese
Salt and pepper

Top, tail and take off some of the skin from the courgettes. Cut into ¼ inch discs. Melt the butter and oil together. When it is smoking lightly, fry the courgettes in batches to a golden brown. Add the tomatoes, garlic, sugar and parsley.

Mix well in and season carefully. Transfer the mixture to a baking dish. Sprinkle all the cheese over it.

Bake at gas mark 7, 425°F (220°C), until hot, brown and bubbling.

Ratatouille

(Stewed tomatoes, onions, courgettes and aubergines)

⅓ pint olive or nut oil
2 large onions, chopped
   coarsely
3 cloves garlic, chopped
2 green peppers and 2 red
   peppers, halved, seeded, cut
   into ¼ inch thick strips
8 large tomatoes, skinned,
   de-seeded and roughly
   chopped

3 large or 6 small aubergines,
   peeled and cut into largish
   chunks
6 courgettes, topped, tailed
   and sliced into ½ inch discs
Salt and pepper
Bouquet garni

Pour the oil into a heavy-bottomed pan. Add the onion. Cover and cook until lightly golden, stirring around to ensure even colouring. Add the garlic. Cook for a minute or so, stirring well. Add the peppers and tomatoes.

In a separate pan quickly fry the aubergines and courgettes in small batches using more oil if necessary until lightly browned.

Add to the main pan. Season lightly with salt and pepper. Add the bouquet garni and cover with a lid. Simmer for an hour, stirring from time to time.

Ratatouille can be served hot or cold.

Aubergine, tuna and tomato mould

Serves 6 to 8 as an *hors d'oeuvre*: 4 to 5 as a main course.

This makes an ideal main course for a summer lunch or a starter or integral part of a buffet. Serve hot or cold.

4 medium but even-sized
   aubergines
   (about 5 inches long)
½ pint plain yoghurt

Salt and pepper
Olive oil for frying
Extra freshly chopped basil
1 × 6 oz tin best tuna fish

For the sauce
2 × 14 oz tins Italian plum
   tomatoes
1 chicken stock cube
1 clove garlic, crushed

1 dash tabasco
1 good sprig basil or 1 tsp
   dried basil
1 tsp sugar

Put all the ingredients for the sauce into a 3 pint heavy-bottomed pan: bring to the boil and simmer until a cohesed pulp is arrived at (a scant ¾ pint when sieved). Press through a fine sieve. Cool. Reserve ⅓ of the sauce for serving.

Meanwhile, cut the aubergines into ¼ inch thick discs, spread the discs on a clean surface, sprinkle lightly with salt, leave for 30 minutes, then rinse under cold water and pat dry with paper towels.

Heat to smoking point a film of olive oil in a large frying pan. Brown the aubergines quickly on both sides, adding more oil when necessary (aubergines absorb a lot, so it is up to you to control this at will) and letting it get very hot before adding more aubergines.

Layer the fried discs in a 2½ pint ovenproof mould (or seamless cake tin), spreading each layer with the tomato sauce and a little yoghurt. Add an extra sprinkling of fresh basil if you like this herb. Halfway through add the flaked tuna in one layer, seasoning lightly.

Cover with a lid or foil: bake at gas mark 5, 375°F (190°C) for 45 to 50 minutes. Unmould and coat with the remaining – heated – sauce. If serving cold leave to cool before unmoulding.

Vegetable marrow with garlic

3 lb marrow
3 oz butter
2 cloves garlic, crushed
1 tsp sugar

1 level tsp powdered bay leaf
Salt and freshly milled black pepper
1 tbsp freshly chopped parsley

Wash the marrow well; cut off the top and tail, then cut into half lengthways. Remove all the pips and pith but do not peel. Cut long, 1 inch-thick strips down the full length; cut each strip into 3 inch sticks.

Melt the butter in a largish pan, add the garlic, then gradually add the marrow sticks, salting and seasoning lightly with pepper, sugar and powdered bay leaf as you go along. Cover the pan with a lid, lower the heat to a minimum and slowly let the juices draw; gently cook the marrow until tender but still somewhat crisp, 5–6 minutes. Add extra seasoning if necessary. Serve the marrow in its juices, sprinkled with the chopped parsley.

18th-century pillow (pilaf) of rice

1 breakfast cup of long grain
  rice
2½ breakfast cups of boiling
  stock (use stock cube)

1 large clove garlic, crushed
1 small onion, finely chopped
2 oz butter

The quantities, timing and temperature for a pilaf must be exact. Do not vary the proportions of stock to rice namely 2½ to 1.

Melt the butter in a frying pan. Soften onion, add garlic, add rice, and fry for 2 minutes, stirring regularly and well. Transfer contents to a lidded, ovenproof pot. Pour over boiling stock.

Cook in pre-heated oven for 20 minutes, gas mark 6, 400°F (200°C). The rice will have soaked up all the stock and will be loose-grained but moist.

Stir in extra butter and Parmesan cheese for a good first course, and when used as a course on its own, a good cupful of each or more of the following can be added at the frying-off stage: sliced mushrooms; prawns; chopped cooked chicken; nuts, raisins; fried bacon striplets; cooked diced vegetables; any herbs and spices you like can be added at will.

Salads

Tudor Salads

It is time we thought once again of the salad bowl as being an artist's palette. As John Evelyn showed us in his Acetaria on 'sallats' we have lost so much, not only in the use of varied ingredients but also in the use of different herbs and dressings.

Here then are six different salads for you to try out. Quantities and combinations I leave entirely to your artistic and creative mood. Whether you serve them as a 'starter', a side dish or a main course is entirely individual. I simply suggest different acidulating agents, aromatics, bases, spices, sweeteners and oils.

Striplets of cold roast beef, ox tongue and sliced onions dressed with oil, vinegar and freshly grated horseradish.

Slices of pear dressed with crushed hazelnuts in a light cream cheese dressing and topped with plenty of chopped chives.

Shredded red cabbage with grapefruit segments dressed with oil, red wine vinegar, orange zest and a little brown sugar.

Peeled and de-seeded cucumber with sliced raw mushrooms dressed with lemon, honey, chopped dill-weed and oil.

Young spinach leaves with striplets of crisply fried bacon, tiny fried bread croutons and a light French dressing mixed with a tablespoon of thick cream.

Cooked rice, diced banana, cubes of cheddar cheese dressed with mayonnaise, orange rind and a hint of curry powder.

Solomongundi (Sallid Magundi)

This Tudor salad is surely England's answer to France's *Salade Niçoise*. It makes a more than substantial main course on a hot summer's day for either lunch outdoors or supper on the terrace.

Cold chicken or turkey
Lettuce
Cold French beans
Anchovy fillets
Green and black grapes
Hard-boiled eggs
Button onions or spring onions

Stoned raisins
Flaked almonds
Oil and vinegar dressing
Plenty of freshly picked and
    chopped green herbs
Lemon rind

As this salad is to be ad-libbed in the way that all salads should be I suggest you start with the chicken or turkey meat as the main ingredient; shred this into striplets and arrange on a bed of lettuce, likewise shredded. Add the rest of the ingredients at will but somewhat abundantly!

Dress liberally with rich oil and vinegar dressing (page 133) which has been spiked with finely grated lemon rind and sprinkle the finished platter with plenty of green herbs. Toss the whole mass together just before serving.

Vegetable salad

A vegetable salad can be the most boring of things or, made as follows, it can be a delicious accompaniment to any cold food.

2 oz carrot	1 oz tiny frozen peas
2 oz potato	Mayonnaise (see page 129)
Salt	Lemon juice

Garnish
Thin anchovy strips
Halves of pimento-stuffed olives

Peel the vegetables, then using a very sharp pointed knife cut these into ⅛ inch slices. Now cut the slices into ⅛ inch strips and finally cut the strips into cubes. All should be the same size as the baby frozen peas.

Cook the carrots in lightly salted water for 2 minutes, no more. Drain, rinse under cold running water and drain again. Do the same with the potatoes. Place all the vegetables on a dry cloth (water-logged vegetables will produce a watery salad). The peas will take no more than one minute. Do not be tempted to cook everything together as each vegetable has a slightly different cooking time. This will keep them crisp.

Dress the diced vegetables in lemon-flavoured mayonnaise. Spread into a flattish dish. Make a lattice of anchovy strips on top, popping a half olive in each diamond created by the lattice.

Salade Niçoise
(Tomato, anchovy and green and red peppers)

There are many versions of this Provençale salad varying from a simple mixture of tomatoes, anchovies and green peppers to elaborations which include tuna fish, hard boiled eggs and even potatoes and, heaven forbid, beetroot (which discolours the whole affair).

Here is my version which appears daily as a main course lunch dish when I am in the South of France.

On a bed of lettuce in a large salad bowl arrange layers of circles of sliced beefsteak or Mediterranean tomatoes, seeded, sliced green and red peppers, quartered artichoke hearts, a few sliced onion rings, pitted black olives, quartered hard-boiled eggs, plenty of anchovy fillets and juicy capers, any freshly-chopped herbs, but if at all possible, plenty of freshly-chopped basil and a good dousing of rich French dressing (page 133) poured over just before serving.

I do add flaked tuna fish (and the oil from the tin) when I serve Salade Niçoise as a main course; and I try to make sure that all the ingredients are well chilled and crisp.

John Evelyn's cucumber salad

A limp lettuce leaf, a wrinkled tomato and a 'dead' egg seem to be the world's idea of an English salad. John Evelyn, the seventeenth-century English diarist, thought very differently. In fact he chose to write a whole tome on the subject of salads in this country; that's food for thought. Here is a charming example:

1 large firm cucumber

Dressing

1 teacup good olive oil	1 tbsp freshly chopped fennel
⅓ cup lemon juice	weed or dill weed (or 1 level
1 tbsp honey	tsp dried dill only – don't
Salt and pepper	use fennel seeds)
	1 tbsp freshly chopped parsley

Using a potato peeler remove the skin from the cucumber. Cut in half lengthways and using a teaspoon remove all the seeds. Cut the cucumber into diagonal pieces ¼ inch thick.

Make up the dressing and dress the salad just before you are going to serve it; if dressed too soon the juices will be drawn and the salad will be too wet. Sprinkle with the parsley and serve either as a side salad or as an inexpensive starter.

Dressed marrow

3 lb marrow
3 tbsp olive oil
Juice of half a lemon

Salt and freshly ground pepper
Lettuce *see* Method

Dressing
3 parts olive oil (¼-pint)
1 part wine vinegar
Dry mustard
Salt and pepper to taste
1 heaped tbsp chopped
   gherkins

1 heaped tbsp capers
1 heaped tbsp shallot or onion,
   finely chopped
1 tbsp chopped parsley

Peel and deseed the marrow and cut into 1 inch cubes.

Melt the oil in a heavy-bottomed pan; put in the marrow, lemon juice and salt and pepper. Cover with a lid and toss over a medium heat until the juices begin to draw. Lower the heat and poach gently until the marrow is just tender. Drain and cool before putting into the refrigerator to chill.

Mix the dressing ingredients, pour over the marrow and serve on a bed of young lettuce leaves or quartered lettuce hearts.

Mushrooms in mustard mayonnaise

12 oz button mushrooms
1 tbsp brandy
3 tbsp water

Squeeze lemon juice
Salt

Dressing
2 tbsp thick bland mayonnaise
   (see page 129)

1 tsp mild French mustard

Quarter the tiny mushrooms (fresh and crisp as possible); put into pan with the brandy, water, lemon juice and a dredge of salt. Toss over a good heat until they are just cooked but still somewhat crisp (it shouldn't take more than a couple of minutes). Drain well reserving the liquor.

Reduce the liquor down to one tablespoonful by boiling rapidly. Pour this into a small dish (or you won't be able to get it out of the pan when it cools). Make up the dressing by blending together the mayonnaise, mustard and mushroom liquor. Add the mushrooms, stir well in and chill well.

Mushroom and chive salad

8 oz button mushrooms
½ lb young spinach leaves

Chives or green tops of spring
   onions

Dressing
4 tbsp olive oil
1 tbsp white wine vinegar
1 level tsp dry mustard

1 tsp sugar
Salt and milled black pepper

Wash, pick and tear into bits the spinach leaves. Arrange on individual plates. Finely slice the raw mushrooms and pile onto the spinach. Make up the dressing, adding plenty of chopped chives. Pour over the salad just before serving.

An interesting version of this salad is to add, at the last moment, some tiny bread croûtons or even white breadcrumbs which have been butter-fried until golden crisp, then cooled. This adds a nice texture to the salad. Add two or three slices of crisply fried streaky bacon and you have yet another version which is more than adequate for a light diet-type lunch.

Melon and cassia bud salad

You may find cassia buds a little hard to get if your local herbalist does not stock them. But they are not dissimilar to cinnamon in flavour, so use the latter if the buds are not available.

1 honeydew melon
4 oz castor sugar
2 tbsp water
Rind of a small orange

1 tsp crushed cassia buds or
   powdered cinnamon
1 tbsp orange flower water

Decoration
Orange segments

Angelica spikes

Put sugar, water, cassia buds or cinnamon, orange flower water and rind into a pan. Simmer until syrupy, but not caramelised. Cut top off melon about 3 inches down. Scoop out the seeds. Then with a melon baller scoop out the flesh (or use a teaspoon).

Put the melon balls into the syrup; leave to cool, then fill back into the melon shell and chill for 4 hours. Decorate with orange segments and angelica spikes.

Bean, tomato and anchovy salad

8 oz tin flageolet beans, drained, rinsed and re-drained
2 × 2 oz tins anchovy fillets
1 small onion, sliced in rings

1 tbsp freshly chopped parsley, basil or marjoram
2 large firm tomatoes, skinned, seeded and chopped
Milk

Dressing
2 tbsp olive oil
2 tbsp lemon juice
1 tsp castor sugar

1 clove garlic, crushed
Oil from anchovies
A little salt if necessary

Drain the oil from the anchovies and reserve for the dressing. Soak the fillets in a little milk for an hour. Take out and cut into half-inch pieces. Combine all the salad ingredients in a bowl. Make up the dressing and mix well in. Turn the salad into a serving dish, sprinkle liberally with the parsley, basil or marjoram and serve as a starter or side salad with cold poached fish.

Avocado and prawn salad

3 large ripe avocado pears
Juice of ½ lemon
4 oz shelled prawns
2 sticks celery, chopped
¼ cucumber, diced

1 cup French dressing (page 133)
1 clove garlic, crushed
1 tbsp chopped parsley
1 tbsp chives or spring onion
1 tsp grated lemon rind

Garnish
2 tomatoes
4 lemon segments

1 hard-boiled egg
Parsley, chopped

Cut two of the pears in half, remove the stones and rub the surface of the flesh with lemon juice. Wrap each half of pear in cling film and refrigerate until ready for use. Peel the third pear, cut in half, pit and then dice the flesh putting it immediately into the dressing to prevent discolouration. Add the rest of the ingredients to the dressing. Mix well and chill. To serve, pile the diced filling into each half shell. Decorate with the tomato, egg and lemon segments. Sprinkle with parsley and stand the pears in avocado dishes or on saucers. Eat with a stainless steel teaspoon.

Rice, herring and gherkin in saffron mayonnaise

4 oz cooked rice
3 rollmop herrings

1 baby onion
1 medium size dill cucumber

Garnish
Dill cucumber
Onion

Parsley, chopped

Dressing
A thimble of saffron
Juice of half a small lemon

Salt and freshly-milled
  white pepper

Trim and cut the herrings into ¼ inch dice. Cut the dill cucumber into equal-sized dice and finely chop the onion. Make up the dressing and bind all the ingredients together. Pile into a serving dish and garnish with discs of dill cucumber and rings of raw onion; sprinkle with parsley.

A salad of neat's tongues

Neat's tongue is Old English for ox or calf tongue. But for this recipe you could also use lamb's tongue.

8 oz piece of cooked tongue
1 medium onion

1 large gherkin
  (dill pickle type)

Dressing
3 tbsp olive oil
1 tbsp lemon juice
1 level tsp lemon rind

Salt, pepper and a touch of
  sugar

Garnish

Chopped parsley	Tomato segments

Slice the tongue, then cut into strips about 2 inches long. Cut onion in half and slice thinly. Cut the gherkin into slices lengthways then strips the same size as the tongue and onions.

Make up the dressing. Toss everything together. Chill well, and serve in small glass bowls garnished with tomato and chopped parsley or on a bed of shredded lettuce.

Savoury sauces and dressings

White sauces
The perfect rich white sauce (Béchamel) 117
Mornay sauce 117
Onion sauce 117
Caper sauce 118
Mushroom sauce 118
Quick cream curry sauce 118
Shrimp sauce 119

Velouté sauces
Basic velouté sauce 119
Chicken stock 119
Fish stock 120
Sauce suprême 120
Sauce Allemande 120
White wine sauce 121

Brown sauces
Basic brown sauce 121
Bordelaise sauce 122
Piquante sauce 122

Hollandaise sauces
Basic Hollandaise sauce 123
Sauce mousseline 124
Maltese sauce 124
Sauce Foyot 124
Choron sauce 124
Sauce Béarnaise 125

Other savoury sauces
Tomato sauce 125
Tomato Madeira sauce 126

White sauces

The perfect rich white sauce (Béchamel)

If you want a velvety-smooth delicately-aromatic creamy sauce, then here it is!

½ pint milk
¾ oz plain white flour
1 oz good butter
1 small piece onion
½ inch piece bay leaf

1 small sprig thyme (or tip of tsp dried)
1 small clove garlic, crushed
Salt and milled white pepper
1 good tbsp thick cream

Allow butter to just melt in small, heavy-bottomed pan. Stir in flour and gradually incorporate the milk (using a small balloon whisk, or a wooden spatula if a non-stick pan is used).

Add rest of ingredients, except cream. Simmer over lowest heat for 10 minutes, stirring from time to time. (You can use a modicum of ordinary, white pepper instead of the freshly milled white pepper but it is very strong. Milled black pepper tastes all right but leaves specks in the sauce.)

Strain into a clean basin, stir in cream and cover with a circle of buttered paper. Stand basin over a pan of simmering water to keep hot until required.

Mornay sauce

To each ½ pint of Rich white sauce add:

2 oz grated cheese
(Gouda, Edam, Cheddar)
1 tsp lemon juice

½ tsp made-up mild French mustard

Serve with macaroni, cauliflower and poached fish.

Onion sauce

To each ½ pint of Rich white sauce use:

4 oz onion
1 oz butter

1 tbsp water
Nutmeg or mace

Slice the onion finely and soften in the butter and water in a lidded pan over a very low heat. Season with a modicum of nutmeg or mace. Put through sieve or blender. Add to sauce.

Serve with roast lamb and with tiny boiled new potatoes.

Caper sauce

To each ½ pint of Rich white sauce add:

1 heaped tbsp capers	A little caper vinegar or lemon juice

Serve with roast lamb, brains, sweetbreads and poached fish.

Mushroom sauce

To each ½ pint of Rich white sauce use:

2 oz white button mushrooms	Mace or nutmeg
1 oz butter	1 tbsp dry Madeira or sherry

Finely slice or chop the mushrooms and quickly fry them in the browned and foaming butter. Season with a modicum of mace or nutmeg and dry Madeira or sherry. Add to sauce. Serve with poached fish, eggs and macaroni (with cheese on top).

Quick cream curry sauce

To each ½ pint of Rich white sauce, add:

1 heaped tsp curry paste	1 tsp chutney
1 tsp apricot jam	

Press through a sieve before serving. Serve with boiled chicken, poached eggs, fish, cauliflower and celery.

Shrimp sauce

To each ½ pint of Rich white sauce, use:

4 oz shrimps or prawns	Lemon juice
1 level tsp mild paprika	Brandy or whisky
Salt	

Shell the frozen or fresh shrimps or prawns. Simmer shells (heads and all) in the Rich white sauce for 20 minutes, together with the paprika. Strain, season with salt, squeeze of lemon juice and a splash of brandy or whisky.

Velouté sauces

Basic velouté sauce

1½ oz flour	1 pint strong chicken or fish stock
3 oz butter	

Melt the butter and gradually stir in the flour. Add the hot stock beating or whisking well until you have a smooth sauce. Simmer for 10 minutes and use appropriately.

Chicken stock

To the skin and bones (not giblets) from a 2½ lb to 3 lb chicken or capon add:

2 carrots	1 bay leaf
1 onion	1 sprig celery leaves
2–3 stalks celery	1 pinch thyme
2 pints water	6 peppercorns

Wash bones in cold water. Roughly chop carcase and vegetables. Put all ingredients into a pan and bring to the boil. Simmer for 1 hour. Keep stock well skimmed. Strain and keep cool until ready for use.

Fish stock

To 2 lb of sole, turbot or bass bones add:

1 small onion	1 sprig parsley
1 carrot	1 bay leaf
1 celery stick	6 white peppercorns
2 oz mushroom stalks and peelings	½ bottle dry white wine
	2 pints cold water
Juice of ½ lemon	Salt

Wash bones well in cold water. Quarter the onion and roughly chop the carrot. Put all ingredients except salt into a large pan and slowly bring to the boil. Simmer for 45 minutes. Strain and cool ready for use.

Add salt half way through cooking but only use a little as you may wish to reduce this stock later, thus increasing its saltiness.

Sauce suprême

To each ¾ pint of Basic velouté sauce add:

¼ pint cream	Juice of ½ small lemon
Salt and pepper	

Whisk in cream and lemon juice and season carefully. It is permissible to add a modicum of yellow colouring to this sauce. But take care that the brand you use is not flavoured. The colouring will enhance the creamy appearance of the sauce.

Serve with boiled chicken, pasta, and poached eggs.

Sauce Allemande

To each ¾ pint of Basic velouté sauce add:

¼ pint cream	Salt and pepper
2 egg yolks	Juice of ½ lemon

Beat the egg yolks into the cream and then whisk into the basic sauce. Add lemon juice and season carefully. Do not boil the sauce after the eggs have been added.

Serve with poached fish, poultry and eggs.

White wine sauce

½ pint fish stock
½ pint dry white wine
2 oz butter
1 oz flour

¼ pint thick cream
Salt
Cayenne pepper
Lemon juice

Mix together the fish stock (page 120) and white wine and reduce to ½ pint by boiling rapidly. Strain through muslin or a napkin.

Melt butter and gradually stir in flour. Beat in boiling stock. Simmer for 15 minutes. Stir in cream and season carefully.

If you want to glaze (brown) this sauce, beat two egg yolks with a little extra cream and whisk into the finished sauce. Do not let the sauce boil once the yolks are added.

Pour over the fish to be glazed and put under a spanking hot grill.

Brown sauces

Basic brown sauce

2 tbsp olive oil
2 oz butter
1 small onion
4 inch carrot
1 celery stalk
2 oz field mushrooms,
  chopped
2 tsp tomato purée
1 chicken stock cube

2 oz flour
1 small bay leaf
1 good pinch of thyme
1 tsp redcurrant jelly
4 fl oz red wine or dry sherry
1½ pints water
Salt and freshly milled black
  pepper

Heat oil and butter until lightly smoking. Allow chopped carrot, celery and onion to gradually brown in this. Add mushrooms and continue to fry over a medium heat. Add tomato purée and, watching carefully as the purée burns easily, allow everything to take on a little more colour. Lower heat, add flour, stir well in and allow to brown stirring from time to time to prevent sticking.

Add herbs now (do not add earlier or they will burn and give a bitter taste). Add redcurrant jelly. Pour mixture into a clean dish whilst you pour into the frying pan the red wine or sherry. This will release any brown sediments on the bottom of the pan. Crumble in the stock cube. Return everything to the pan. Add the water, bring to the boil, adding a little (½ tsp) salt and pepper.

Simmer for 30 minutes, stirring to prevent sticking. Strain the sauce into a clean pan (you should have about 1 pint of sauce when it is finished). Adjust the seasoning with more salt if necessary. Cover with a circle of buttered paper and keep hot over simmering water until required.

This sauce can be frozen in small quantities.

Bordelaise sauce

To each ½ pint of Basic brown sauce add:

1 small onion	1 oz butter or 2 tbsp oil
2 oz mushrooms	

Fry the finely chopped onion and mushrooms in the butter or oil. This sauce classically is strained and contains a garnish of beef marrow. This refinement is entirely optional.

Serve with grilled steaks and chops, roast duckling, chicken or turkey.

Piquante sauce

To each ½ pint of Basic brown sauce add:

4 tbsp red wine vinegar	1 tbsp finely chopped parsley
1 tbsp finely chopped shallot or onion	1 tbsp capers
1 tbsp finely chopped gherkins	

Simmer the finely-chopped onion in the wine vinegar until the onion is soft. Add the finely chopped capers, gherkins and parsley.

Serve with grilled meats and deep-fried chicken.

Hollandaise Sauces

Basic Hollandaise sauce

2 tbsp white wine vinegar	3 egg yolks
3 tbsp water	6 oz unsalted butter
1 small piece onion	Lemon juice
6 peppercorns	Salt and freshly ground
1 small piece bay leaf	white pepper

Put the butter into a small pan and stand this in a warm place to melt and get quite hot. Put the wine vinegar, water, onion, peppercorns and bay leaf into a small pan and boil rapidly until the mixture is reduced to 1 tablespoon.

Now add two more tablespoons of water (you require the original quantity of liquid to extract the aromas in the first stage; you then need to replace some of the liquid which has evaporated).

Select a bowl which has a good round bottom and which will sit in the top of a pan of boiling water. Put the egg yolks into the bowl and strain the liquid on to them, stirring well with a tiny balloon whisk or spatula.

Arrange the bowl over the boiling water and whisk gently, but completely, taking care to see that the egg doesn't set on the sides of the bowl.

Continue whisking until the mixture is thick and the whisk leaves a definite trail, but stop before the eggs scramble! (Have a container of cold water to hand as a safety precaution. Dip the base of the bowl into the water to remove the residual heat quickly, thus avoiding any possibility of the egg over-cooking.)

Now stand the bowl on a folded damp cloth (this helps keep the bowl steady as you whisk). Whisk in a few drops only of the melted butter at first and as the sauce thickens add the butter more quickly until it is all incorporated (leave out the milky sediment which will have settled to the bottom of the pan whilst the butter has been slowly melting).

Adjust the seasoning, adding a little lemon juice and salt and pepper if you think it is needed. Put little pieces of butter over the surface to prevent a crust forming. The butter can be whisked briskly into the sauce just before serving. Stand the sauce in a warm place until you are ready to use it.

As this is a warm sauce, it must not be kept where it is too hot or it will separate, so keep an eye on it. A good place to put it is on top of a plate which in turn is standing on top of a pan of hot, but not simmering, water.

Serve with any boiled or steamed vegetables, poached fish, hot fish mousses and soufflés, hot asparagus and hot artichokes.

Sauce mousseline

To the Basic Hollandaise sauce add:

⅓ pint double or whipping cream

Half whip the cream before adding to the sauce.

Serve with any dish where Hollandaise sauce could be served.

Maltese sauce

Use the Basic Hollandaise sauce but substitute orange juice for lemon juice and add 1 teaspoon of carefully grated orange rind and a hint of mace to the finished sauce.

Serve with any dish where Hollandaise sauce could be served.

Sauce Foyot

To the Basic Hollandaise sauce add:

1 tsp finely chopped or crushed garlic	1 tbsp chopped tarragon
	1 tbsp chopped parsley

Serve with poached or grilled fish, artichokes and grilled meats.

Choron sauce

To the Basic Hollandaise sauce add:

1 dsp mild tomato purée	1 dsp chopped tarragon

Serve with any dish where Hollandaise Sauce could be served.

Sauce Béarnaise

I put Sauce Béarnaise in this section for it is identical in make-up to Hollandaise sauce but with a tarragon flavour. To make Sauce Béarnaise follow the recipe for Hollandaise but make the following changes:

At the 'reduction' stage, crumble into the liquid half a chicken stock cube (use Knorr or Maggi which are less potent than other brands). This is as good as the meat glaze called for in the traditional French recipe for Béarnaise.

Substitute tarragon vinegar for wine vinegar.

Finish the sauce with a dessertspoon each of chopped tarragon and/or parsley.

Don't add salt until the end as the stock cube may well suffice.

Serve with grilled fillet steak, baby lamb cutlets, grilled or deep-fried fish.

Other savoury sauces

Tomato sauce

2 lb tomatoes
1 tbsp tomato purée
1 small onion
1 clove garlic
2 rashers unsmoked bacon
½ pint stock (from stock cube)
½ oz white flour

1 oz butter
¼ tsp grated lemon rind
¼ tsp powdered rosemary
1 tsp lemon juice
1 small glass medium sherry
1 tsp brown sugar
Salt and freshly milled pepper

Heat butter in a heavy-bottomed pan. Fry strips of bacon and chopped onion until lightly browned. Stir in tomato purée (you could use ketchup), watching carefully as purée burns easily.

Stir in flour and add all seasonings (crush the garlic). Add sherry, stock, lemon juice, and the tomatoes, skinned and de-seeded.

Simmer for 20 minutes until sauce is bright and shiny. Press through hair sieve, correct consistency, adjusting with more stock. Salt and sugar to your taste.

Re-heat before serving.

If a creamy sauce is required, add ¼ pint double cream after the sieving stage.

Serve with poached and grilled fish, poultry, ravioli, gnocchi, cannelloni, fish cakes and grilled sausage.

Tomato Madeira sauce

This is delicious for roast lamb, turkey, duck or chicken.

Make the modest amount of sauce in a large (6 pint) pan. It's easier and you will get a better result.

1 oz butter or olive oil for frying
1 medium (3 oz) onion, chopped
1 medium (3 oz) carrot cut into small dice
1 oz mushrooms cut into dice
1 heaped dsp tomato purée
1 heaped tsp (half a good ounce) flour
1 level tsp mild paprika
¼ pint red wine

¼ pint dry Madeira
1 pint strong chicken stock (made from chicken bones or use 1½ stock cubes)
8 oz fresh tomatoes, skinned, seeded and roughly chopped
Salt if needed
Extra dry or medium dry Madeira

Melt the butter or oil letting it take on an almond flavour and golden colour. Add the onion and carrot, lower heat and brown, stirring regularly.

Add the mushroom and mix in the purée, letting it take on a little colour – but it must not burn. Sprinkle over the flour, stir in well and allow to colour for a minute, stirring all the time. Add the paprika.

Turn the mixture onto a dinner plate, turn up the heat and pour in the red wine. Work all the residues from the bottom of the pan into the wine.

Add the Madeira, stock, tomatoes and the fried vegetable mixture. Bring everything to the boil. Reduce the heat, simmer the sauce for 30 minutes, when you will have approximately 1 pint of sauce. Strain into a clean pan through a fine meshed strainer. Leave to cool. Refrigerate until needed. (This sauce can be made two days in advance).

To serve Bring the sauce to the boil. Add a small glass of dry or medium dry Madeira, strain again into a sauce boat and serve. The sauce can be further enriched by whisking in 1 oz of fridge-hard French or Dutch butter cut into cubes immediately after re-heating, but before pouring into sauce boat. Once the butter is whisked in, the sauce should not be boiled.

Curry sauce

This is a basic curry sauce which can be adapted to all sorts of uses and can be served either hot or cold.

1 onion	4 cloves
1 heaped tsp curry powder	½ bay leaf
1 tsp tomato purée	1 crushed clove garlic
½ oz flour	2 tbsp brandy (optional)
½ pint chicken stock	Salt and freshly ground pepper
1 dsp apricot purée or jam	Oil for frying
1 dsp sultanas	Mayonnaise (page 129) if serving cold

Chop the onion and fry in 2 tablespoons of oil until golden brown. Add the curry powder and cook for 1 minute, stirring well. Add the tomato purée and then the flour.

Reduce the heat and let a crust form on the bottom of the pan (this will give both colour and flavour to the sauce). Remove the mixture from the pan and swill the bottom with brandy or a little stock, incorporating any crust. Return the mixture to the pan and add the stock and other ingredients. Bring to the boil and sim-mer for 20 minutes.

Strain into a basin and leave to cool, covered with an oiled paper.

If you wish to use the sauce cold for a chicken mayonnaise dish or to use with cold poached fish, add half as much again of thick mayonnaise and stir well in. If the sauce looks too thick, add a little lemon juice and a touch of cold water.

If you want a hot, creamy sauce for boiled chicken with rice, or noisettes of veal, add ¼ pint double cream and bring the sauce back to the boil.

Bread sauce

This sauce can be the dull stodgy stuff frequently served in restaurants in England, or the very refined sauce I give below:

½ pint milk
2 oz butter
1 small onion
½ clove garlic
1 bay leaf or a little grated
  nutmeg or 2 cloves

Salt and freshly milled white
  pepper
3 oz fresh white breadcrumbs
¼ pint single cream
A little chicken stock or extra
  milk

Put the milk, butter, garlic, bay leaf (nutmeg or cloves) and onion into the top of a double saucepan and make the mixture as hot as possible. Add the breadcrumbs and let the sauce cook until it is quite thick and smooth. Pass the entire contents of the pan through a blender, Mouli or hair-sieve.

Add the cream, adjust the seasoning, re-heat and serve.

If the sauce is too thick (this will depend on the kind of bread you use) thin it down with a little white stock or milk.

If the sauce has to be kept hot, return it to the double saucepan after sieving and cover with a circle of buttered paper to prevent a skin forming. Keep the water in the bottom pan hot.

Serve with roast chicken, turkey, grilled sausage and rissoles.

Cumberland sauce

1 lb redcurrant jelly
¼ pint ruby port
3 oranges
3 lemons
1 level dsp dry mustard

1 small onion
Salt
Tip of tsp powdered mace
1 sherry glass cider vinegar

Using a potato peeler, remove the rind from all six pieces of fruit. Care must be taken to ensure that no white pith is taken off with the rind, as this is the bitter part of citrus fruits.

Collect the strips of rind together into manageable piles and with a very sharp, thin-spined knife shred the rind as finely as you possibly can – try to shred it as fine as a pin, for this will ensure that your sauce is good-looking and elegant. (Patience at this stage will pay dividends.)

Put the shredded peel into a pan and pour over enough water

to cover it. Bring the contents of the pan to the boil and immediately pour into a strainer. Cool the peel under running cold water for a minute or so, then put on one side to drain.

Finely chop the onion. Squeeze and strain the juice of two of the oranges and two lemons. Bring this to the boil with all the remaining ingredients and simmer for 15 minutes over a low heat, stirring to ensure that the jelly melts evenly and doesn't burn. (Always use ruby port rather than tawny as this gives a good colour.)

Add the shredded rind and boil for a further 5 to 10 minutes until the sauce starts to thicken. Cool, then refrigerate until the sauce is somewhat jellied. Serve chilled and do not strain.

Serve with cold roast meats, galantines, and terrines.

Mayonnaise

Basic mayonnaise

½ pint nut oil
½ pint olive oil
6 egg yolks
1 tsp dry mustard

1 tbsp wine vinegar
Cold water
Salt and freshly ground white pepper

Put the yolks into a round-bottomed basin. This is essential as you need to collect and control the yolks within a small area. Add the salt, mustard and a little pepper and work these with a balloon whisk, or more laboriously with a wooden spoon, until they are really thick and sticky. (This recipe is not suitable for a blender.)

Have the oil in a jug; then by first using a teaspoon, add drops of oil to the egg mixture, whisking vigorously. Beat each drop well in before adding the next few drops. It is essential to take care in the early stages of mayonnaise making – if you are meticulous at the beginning, you will have no trouble later.

After the first tablespoonful or so of oil has been added you can start to add the oil more quickly – experience will teach you just when this can be done. As soon as the emulsion starts to reject the oil (this is quite different from curdling) add a little vinegar and beat until it is creamy again. Mayonnaise is curdled when the yolks and oil are flecked and liquid instead of creamy. If this happens you must start again with a single egg yolk and work the curdled mayonnaise into it drop by drop. Sometimes a tablespoon of boiling water added to the curdled mayonnaise will do the trick.

Keep the mayonnaise as stiff as your arm will allow! If you have a strong arm you will be able to make mayonnaise as thick as butter, which could be cut with a knife. If the mayonnaise is too thick thin it down with single cream, vinegar or cold water (or a combination of all three); water gives a blander result than vinegar, cream adds richness.

The finished mayonnaise can be flavoured with ketchup, sherry, lemon juice, brandy or Worcester sauce.

Store mayonnaise in a cool, but not cold, place. It does not keep indefinitely, but will be quite all right for four or five days. If it begins to look oily, just add a tablespoonful of boiling water and whisk until it is creamy again.

Remoulade sauce (quick method)

To each ½ pint of Mayonnaise add:

1 heaped tbsp finely chopped piccalilli	1 dsp chopped parsley

Serve with deep-fried crumbed fillets of plaice or goujons of sole.

Green mayonnaise

To each ½ pint of Mayonnaise add:

1 large bunch watercress	1 tbsp chopped tarragon
1 tbsp chopped parsley	Squeeze of lemon juice
1 tbsp chopped chervil or chives	Salt

Pick the watercress leaves and plunge into boiling salted water for 3–4 minutes. Run under cold water to cool. Drain very well pressing to remove all liquid. Chop and blend this with the Mayonnaise (this is best done in a blender). Add the herbs and lemon juice.

Dried herbs will not do for this bright green sauce but 1 teaspoon of onion juice can be substituted for the chives or chervil.

Serve with cold fish pâtés, grilled or poached salmon, cold poached eggs.

Tartare sauce

To each ½ pint of stiff Mayonnaise add:

1 dsp chopped capers	1 dsp chopped parsley
1 dsp chopped gherkins	Squeeze of lemon juice
1 dsp chopped shallot or onion	Salt and pepper *see* Method

Adjust consistency with water or thin cream if necessary. Only add salt and pepper if the sauce needs it for your taste.

Serve with grilled or deep-fried fish, fish cakes.

Gribiche sauce

To each ½ pint of Tartare sauce add 1 finely chopped hard-boiled egg.

Serve as an alternative to Tartare Sauce.

Cocktail sauce

To each ½ pint of stiff Mayonnaise add:

1 dsp tomato purée (or ketchup)	1 large tsp lemon juice
1 tsp Worcester sauce	1 large tsp brandy

Fold in a tablespoon of stiffly beaten cream for extra richness.

Use for dressing shrimps, prawns, and crab cocktails.

Aioli (Garlic mayonnaise) Pronounce this sauce 'I-o-lee'.

To each ½ pint of stiff Mayonnaise add:

Lemon juice	8 cloves garlic

Pound the garlic to a paste. If you don't have a mortar and pestle, this can be done in a blender or by using the butt of a rolling pin. Add to the mayonnaise with lemon juice to taste.

Small spoonfuls of this sauce can be added at table to such soups as fish, tomato, celery and vegetable, giving a warming touch.

This garlic sauce can also be served with any raw vegetables as an appetiser or hors d'oeuvre. The raw vegetables, or crudités, are cut into attractive and manageable pieces and served in a large bowl of crushed ice (or even ice cubes and water) to keep them crisp and fresh.

The vegetables can be prepared the morning or day before a party and packed into plastic bags (keeping each vegetable separate). Chill but do not freeze.

Suggested vegetables are: carrot sticks; cauliflower florets; cucumber sticks (deseeded but not peeled); whole radishes; fennel or celery sticks; tiny button mushrooms; baby new potatoes, cooked; green or red peppers, deseeded and cut into strips; celeriac, cut into thin sticks.

Old English salad cream

1 tbsp flour	4 tsp mustard
½ tbsp pepper	4 oz sugar
1 egg	1 pint milk
4 tsp salad oil	½ pint white vinegar or ¼ pint
1 tsp salt	brown vinegar

Mix all dry ingredients together, add oil. Beat the egg well into the milk and then gradually mix with the dry ingredients. Add vinegar slowly and then thicken by heating in a double boiler or in a bowl over a saucepan of boiling water, stirring all the time.

Bottle when cold.

Serve (as used to be the custom in England between the wars) with delicious cold poached salmon.

Basic vinaigrette sauce (French dressing)

6 tbsp olive oil
½ tsp mustard
2 tbsp red or white wine
vinegar

¼ tsp castor sugar
Salt and freshly milled pepper
1 clove garlic (optional)

Finely chop the garlic (see below). Put all the ingredients into a screw-top jar and shake until completely blended.

Vinaigrette sauce keeps almost indefinitely in a screw-top jar. Do not add garlic and herbs until ready for use.

Basic marinade

To make 1 pint of marinade.

1 large onion
1 large carrot
1 large clove garlic
1 teacup red or dry white wine
½ teacup red or white wine
vinegar

½ teacup olive oil
1 bay leaf
1 dozen peppercorns
Salt and pepper

Very thinly slice the onion and carrot. Lightly salt and pepper the meat or fish to be marinated. Place the meat in your dish and mix with the vegetables, crushed and chopped garlic, crushed bay leaf and peppercorns. In a pan warm the oil, vinegar and wine. Pour over the rest of the ingredients.

Leave meat to marinate in the refrigerator for one or two days, turning and basting every three or four hours.

Sweet Sauces

Rich apple sauce 135
Apricot sauce 135
Raspberry sauce 135
Caramel sauce 136
Orange sauce 136
Rich dark chocolate sauce 136
Hot chocolate sauce 137
Sour cream sauce 137
Vanilla apricot sauce (hot or cold) 137
English custard 138
Specially rich rum sauce 138
Lemon cream sauce 139
Michael Smith's special syrup for fruit salads 139

Rich apple sauce

This recipe restores apple sauce to its former Tudor glory.

4 Cox's apples
1 tbsp castor sugar
1 oz unsalted butter

1 oz ground almonds
  (optional)
2 tbsp water (or orange juice)

Peel, quarter, core and slice the apples. Melt the butter and sugar in the water or juice. Add the apples.

Simmer in a lidded pan until soft. Stir in the almonds and either blend, or press through a hair-sieve.

Re-heat carefully or serve cold with roast pork, duckling or sausages.

Apricot sauce

4 oz can apricot halves or
  2 tbsp apricot jam
1 oz sugar

2 tbsp Grand Marnier, Kirsch
  or Amaretto

Drain the apricots, retaining 2 tablespoons of the syrup. Put all ingredients together in a pan. Simmer for 5 minutes. Blend or press through a hair-sieve.

If you want a tangier sauce add 1 tablespoon of lemon juice instead of the liqueurs.

Serve, either hot or cold, with hot sponge puddings, baked bananas, rice pudding and ice cream.

Raspberry sauce

8 oz fresh or frozen
  raspberries
Juice of 1 lemon

3 oz castor sugar
12 tbsp gin or water

Bring all the ingredients to the boil over a very low heat. Simmer gently for 5 minutes and then very gently press the contents through a fine sieve, applying only a minimum of pressure to the fruit so that the sauce remains clear. If you wish you can serve the sauce without sieving.

Serve, either hot or cold, over pineapple, melon, sponge pudding (particularly chocolate pudding) ice creams and melbas.

Caramel sauce

3 oz castor sugar
3 tbsp warm water

¼ pint half-whipped double cream

Put sugar into aluminium pan (not enamel lined as the heat will crack the enamel). Allow sugar to caramelise slowly.

Cover your hand with a cloth or oven glove and pour in the water (it will splutter and splash). Stir and allow to boil until syrupy. Cool, then stir in the whipped cream. Chill well.

Serve with caramelled pears or oranges, sponge pudding and ice cream.

Orange sauce

½ pint orange juice (bottled, tinned or fresh)
1 tsp orange rind
1 oz castor sugar

1½ oz unsalted butter
1 oz plain white flour
¼ pint double cream

Melt butter, stir in flour, gradually add orange juice, allow to boil. Add sugar to taste and orange rind, simmer for 5 minutes. Add cream (do not use milk as this will curdle), bring to boil again and serve.

If serving cold, sprinkle surface with castor sugar to prevent skin forming.

Serve, hot or cold, with pies and puddings.

Rich dark chocolate sauce

There is no way you will arrive at this type of chocolate-lover's sauce if you don't use a good brand of chocolate. I suggest Menier, Cadbury's Bournville, Terry's Bitter, or Rowntree's.

6 oz chocolate broken into pieces

⅓ pint water
4 oz castor sugar

Put the chocolate in a basin over simmering water and let it melt. Stir in the water, add the sugar, and continue to let this heat until all is dissolved and smooth. Cool, then refrigerate.

This should be a thinnish sauce – about as thin as single cream – but this will depend on the type of chocolate you have used: if it is too thick melt it down again over hot water and add a little more water. If you stir in water when it's cold it will go creamy and not be the dark glossy sauce you are looking for.

Hot chocolate sauce

3½ oz bitter chocolate	2 egg yolks
⅛ pint water	1 oz castor sugar
1 tsp vanilla essence	½ oz unsalted butter

Break chocolate into pieces and put in basin over boiling water together with sugar, essence, water and butter. Stir occasionally and allow to get quite hot. Remove basin from water and whisk in the two beaten egg yolks.

If you want a cold sauce, leave to cool and if too thick whisk in a little water to slacken the consistency. Serve hot with profiteroles and sponge puddings or cold with gâteaux and ice cream.

Sour cream sauce

½ pint sour cream	¼ tsp nutmeg
2 oz castor sugar	¼ tsp cinnamon
1 small lemon	¼ pint double cream

Grate the rind of the lemon and stir into sour cream. Add the sugar, nutmeg and cinnamon. Whip the double cream and using a slotted spoon fold in the sour cream mixture. Chill well.

Good with hot and cold fruit pies and puddings.

Vanilla apricot sauce (hot or cold)

4 fl oz water	1 tsp vanilla essence (or use
2 oz castor sugar	vanilla sugar if you have it to
8 oz apricot jam	hand)

Bring the sugar, essence and water to the boil and simmer until clear.

In a second smaller pan, put in the jam and half the syrup. Then, stirring all the time, bring to the boil over a low heat. Press through a hair-sieve, adjust the consistency using more of the syrup. (If the sauce is to be served cold, you will find it will require more syrup, added when quite cold.)

Lemon juice, rum, Kirsch or any liqueur can be added for further interest.

English custard

4 eggs	1 pint milk
2 oz castor sugar	1 tsp of vanilla essence
1 tsp cornflour	

Cream the eggs, sugar and cornflour. Bring the milk to the boil, add the essence, pour over the egg mixture whisking briskly all the time. If the sauce doesn't thicken immediately, return the mixture to the pan and place over a *minimum* heat, and, stirring all the time, bring the sauce just to boiling point when it will thicken.

Have your sink half-filled with cold water into which you can plunge the bottom of the pan to remove any residual heat which may be sufficient to curdle the custard.

Specially rich rum sauce

½ pint sweet white wine	2 oz castor sugar
3 tbsp Jamaican rum	Rind of 1 lemon
5 egg yolks	

Cream the egg yolks and sugar until every granule of sugar has dissolved. Remove the rind of the lemon with a potato peeler or with a sharp knife, patiently shred this as fine as hair. Add to the egg yolks and stir in the wine and rum.

Arrange the basin over a pan of boiling water, making sure the water is in contact with the bottom of the basin. Whisk the sauce slowly, but continuously until it is as thick as double cream. Remove from the heat and continue whisking until the heat has diminished somewhat.

Keep the sauce warm over a pan of hot, but not boiling water. This time the water must not be in contact with the bottom of the basin.

Ideal with Christmas Pudding, vanilla sponge, a special apple pie or with ice cream.

Lemon cream sauce

4 oz lemon curd or lemon cheese

¼ pint single cream

Mix the two ingredients together and heat through over a low heat until hot but not boiling. Pour into a warm sauceboat and serve.

Michael Smith's special syrup for fruit salads

2 navel oranges
2 lemons
1 lime
1 sherry glass Kirsch, Akvavit or gin

8 oz castor sugar
½ pint water

Remove the rind from the citrus fruits with a potato peeler. Shred very finely. (You will not need to use the flesh or juice.)

Put rind, sugar and water into a pan. Simmer until a light syrupy consistency. Cool and add the liqueur. Chill until required.

Spoon over any fresh fruits just before serving.

The juice from the citrus fruits may be used elsewhere or, if you are making a fresh fruit salad, the salad fruits may be soaked in the juices before pouring the Special syrup over at the last minute.

Butters: savoury and sweet

Savoury butters

Use these on top of grilled meats, fish or sausages and to add interest to plain boiled vegetables.

Anchovy butter

4 oz butter
1 crushed clove garlic
12 anchovy fillets

Lemon juice
Touch of cayenne pepper
Black pepper

Cream the butter, add all the other ingredients, season to taste but do not add any salt. Pass through a blender or Mouli and then a hair-sieve. Form into a roll and fold in wetted greaseproof paper or foil. Refrigerate until needed.

Parsley butter

4 oz butter
2 tbsp freshly chopped parsley
1 tsp chopped chives

Lemon juice
Salt and freshly ground white
  pepper

Cream the butter, add the parsley and chives, season with lemon juice, salt and pepper. Form into a roll as in preceding recipe and refrigerate.

Garlic butter

4 oz butter
4 cloves garlic
1 tbsp lemon juice

Salt and freshly ground white
  pepper
1 dash tabasco sauce

Cream the butter, add the crushed garlic, season to taste with lemon juice, salt and tabasco. Form into a roll, wrap in grease-proof paper and refrigerate.

Tomato butter

4 oz butter
2 heaped tsp tomato purée
Squeeze of lemon juice

Good pinch mace, nutmeg, or
  dried rosemary
Salt and pepper

Cream the butter, and add the tomato purée, lemon juice, seasoning and spices. Rub through a hair-sieve and form into a roll.

Herb butter

---

4 oz butter	1 tsp chopped chives
1 tsp chopped parsley	Half crushed clove garlic
1 tsp chopped fennel fronds	Lemon juice
1 tsp chopped chervil	Salt and pepper
1 tsp chopped basil	

Use freshly picked and chopped herbs. Cream the butter, beat in the garlic and herbs, season to taste with lemon juice, salt and pepper. Form into a roll and refrigerate.

Watercress butter

---

1 bunch watercress	1 pinch castor sugar
2 oz butter	Salt and pepper
1 tsp lemon juice	

Use fresh, crisp watercress. Pick all the leaves from the stalks, then either put all the ingredients into a blender or pound with the butt of a rolling pin in a metal basin. Rub the finished butter through a hair-sieve and form into a roll.

Nut butter (Beurre noisette)

---

4 oz butter

Melt the butter in a pan and let it foam. At the moment it begins to give off an almondy nutty flavour, pour immediately over grilled fish or poached eggs.

Black butter (Beurre noir)

---

4 oz butter	½ tsp cracked white (or black)
Juice of ½ lemon	peppercorns
Salt	

Swirl butter round in heavy bottomed pan until it passes the nut butter stage (see above). Do not allow the butter to burn, season to taste. Add lemon juice, to arrest the browning process.

Sweet butters

Use these to vary your sandwiches or cakes, or on pancakes or waffles.

Hazelnut butter

4 oz unsalted butter
2 oz toasted hazelnuts

1 tsp brown sugar

Cream butter and sugar. Beat in the finely-crushed nuts and form into roll.

Cinnamon butter

4 oz unsalted butter
2 oz brown sugar

1 tsp powdered cinnamon
1 tbsp rum (optional)

Cream butter and sugar. Beat in the cinnamon and rum. Form into roll.

Brandy or rum butter

4 oz unsalted butter
4 oz castor or brown sugar
4 tbsp brandy or rum

1 tsp lemon or orange juice
½ tsp grated lemon or orange rind
1 tbsp boiling water

Cut the butter into 1 inch cubes and put with the sugar and lemon rind into a basin. Beat until creamy, add the boiling water, and continue to beat until every grain of sugar has been dissolved. Add the lemon juice and brandy and beat well in. Put into lidded wax cartons and store in the refrigerator until ready for use.

This butter can safely be made two or three weeks in advance, and should by no means be restricted to Christmas puddings. I use white sugar and lemon for brandy butter, but brown sugar and orange for rum butter. Brandy or rum butter is good served with hot pies and sponge puddings.

Orange or lemon butter

4 oz butter
Finely grated zest of 1 orange
  or 1 lemon (heaped tsp)
Salt and pepper or icing sugar

Good squeeze orange or
  lemon juice
Pinch mace

Cream the butter, add the zest of the fruit and the juice, add the mace, season and rub through sieve and form into a roll.

Where this is used for sweet sandwiches, omit salt and pepper and blend in 1 teaspoon icing sugar and use unsalted butter.

Walnut butter

4 oz unsalted butter
2 oz finely crushed or ground
  walnuts

1 tsp brown sugar
Pinch nutmeg
Squeeze lemon juice

Cream the butter, add the walnuts, brown sugar, nutmeg and lemon juice. Rub through sieve and form into a roll.

Honey butter

4 oz unsalted butter
2 oz well-flavoured honey

Squeeze lemon juice
1 tsp rose-water

Cream the butter, add the honey, the lemon juice and the rose-water. Rub through sieve and form into a roll.

Sweets and puddings

Steamed puddings

Guard's pudding

Serves 5 or 6

I wonder to which generation readers belong who enjoy this very typical English steamed pudding, said to be a great favourite with Her Majesty's gentlemen of the Guards: it was considered too good for the other ranks! I hazard, however, that if you make it on a crisp, cold day a new generation of camp followers will be initiated.

6 oz brown breadcrumbs	3 good tbsp raspberry jam
6 oz suet	1 large egg, beaten
4 oz Demerara sugar	Juice and rind of 1 large lemon
1 level tsp bicarbonate of soda	

Mix together all the dry ingredients. Mix in the jam, lemon juice and rind, and finally the beaten egg. Well butter a 2–2½ pint pudding basin. Place a buttered circle of paper in the bottom. Spoon in the mixture which will be fairly stiff. Cover the basin with well-buttered foil, allowing a good inch pleat across the top. Tie down firmly, making a handle across the top of the basin for ease of lifting. Steam for 2½ hours over well-rolling water, remembering to top up the pan with boiling water from time to time.

Remove the foil, run a knife around between the pudding and basin, and turn out on to a warm plate.

Serve with custard (dare I say it – the commercial kind, made by Buzby's cousin!), or with raspberry sauce (see page 135).

This pudding is not meant in any way to be refined: maybe that's why good honest folk like it so much!

Black treacle 'duff'

Serves 5 or 6

For those who find black treacle too powerful – but I doubt if they will if they are lovers of suet duffs – then brown treacle, difficult to get, or golden syrup can be substituted.

8 oz self-raising flour
2 oz suet
2 oz hard, cold butter, grated
1 heaped tsp grated lemon rind

1 egg
Juice of 1 lemon, made up to ⅓ pint with water
Approx 6 oz black treacle or syrup

Using good butter, well grease a 3 pint pudding basin (make sure it fits the steamer). Toss the flour with the suet, grated butter and lemon rind. Beat the egg and add to the lemon juice and water. Mix into the flour mixture at one fell swoop. Gather the mixture into a soft dough. Divide the dough into four portions, each a little larger than the next. Press – don't roll – the dough into four circles which will fit the basin in layers.

Put the smallest circle into the base of the basin. Spoon over it a tablespoon of treacle. Fit the rest of the circles, alternating with a good spoonful of treacle, ending with a top of suet dough. Cover the basin with well-buttered foil, allowing a good inch pleat across the top. Tie down firmly, making a handle across the top of the basin for ease of lifting. Steam at a good rolling boil for 2½ hours, topping up the pan with *boiling* water as and when necessary.

Remove the foil, run a palette knife around between the basin and the pudding and turn out on to a warm plate.

Serve with custard. I always pass lemon segments as well to contrast with the sweetness of the treacle.

Chocolate sponge pudding with apples

Serves 6

2 small apples
1 oz butter
1 tbsp lemon juice
(The first three ingredients are
   optional: raspberry jam can
   be substituted)
4 oz castor sugar

4 oz unsalted butter
2 medium eggs, beaten
2 oz cocoa
4 oz self-raising flour
1 oz ground almonds
3 tbsp cream-type sherry (or
   fresh milk)

Peel and core the apples; cut into small pieces. Melt the butter with the lemon juice in a small pan, cook the apples in this until tender. Mash roughly with a fork. Leave to cool.

Sieve the flour and cocoa together. Cream the unsalted butter and sugar until fluffy. Gradually beat in the eggs. Beat in the ground almonds, then fold in the flour and cocoa adding enough sherry or milk to give a soft dropping consistency.

Well butter a 2 pint basin or six individual dariole tins. Put the apples or raspberry jam into the bottom. Spoon in the mixture. Cover with buttered, pleated foil, tie down and steam for 2 hours (large basin), 1½ hours (individual tins).

Serve with Hot chocolate sauce (page 137), ice-cream, cream, custard (page 138) or Raspberry sauce (page 135).

Coffee, walnut and date pudding

Serves 5 or 6

4 oz castor sugar
4 oz unsalted butter
2 eggs, beaten
1 level tsp instant coffee,
   dissolved in 1 tbsp of boiling
   water and cooled

4 oz self-raising flour, sieved
2 oz walnuts, roughly chopped
2 oz dates, roughly chopped
   and soaked in 1 tbsp rum

Well butter a 2 pint pudding basin or mould. Put a small circle of buttered paper in the bottom.

Cream the butter and sugar until light and fluffy. Beat in the eggs a little at a time: add the dissolved coffee. Fold in the sieved flour, then the nuts and dates and the modest amount of rum.

Spoon the mixture into the basin. Level the top. Cover with buttered foil, making an inch pleat and tying down firmly.

Steam for 2 hours over gently rolling water. Top up the pan at frequent intervals with boiling water from a kettle. Remove the foil, run a palette knife round the sides of the basin, and turn out onto a warm serving dish. Remove the disc of paper.

Serve with Vanilla apricot sauce (see page 137), thick cream or English custard (see page 138).

Tangy lemon sponge pudding

Serves 5 or 6

This pudding is truly lemony.

4 oz unsalted butter	Juice of 2 lemons
4 oz castor sugar	Cold water
2 large eggs, beaten	1 slice lemon
Grated rind of 2 lemons	1 tbsp lemon cheese or lemon
5 oz self-raising flour	curd
1 level tsp baking powder	

Cream the butter and sugar until light and fluffy. Beat in the eggs gradually. Add the rind. Sieve the flour and baking powder, and gradually fold into the mixture, incorporating well and using the lemon juice to mix to a soft dropping consistency and a little cold water if necessary. (This will depend on the size of the eggs used.)

Well butter a 2½ to 3 pint basin. Place the slice of lemon in the base. Spoon the lemon cheese over it. Spoon in the mixture. Cover with buttered foil, making a good pleat across the top. Tie down firmly with string, making a loose handle over the top of the basin for ease of lifting the basin out of the steamer.

Steam at a good roll for 1½ hours, and turn out as for previous steamed puddings.

Serve with Lemon cream sauce (see page 139).

Vanilla sponge pudding

Serves 4 or 5

2 eggs
Unsalted butter
Vanilla sugar or sugar and 2
 tsp vanilla essence

Self-raising flour
2 tsp cold water

Weigh the eggs and use the same amount of butter, sugar and flour, (i.e., if the eggs weigh 4 oz, use 4 oz butter, 4 oz sugar and 4 oz flour). Have the butter at room temperature, add the sugar and beat until every granule of sugar has disappeared. Add 1 teaspoonful of the flour and beat in well.

Beat the eggs with the cold water and gradually beat them into the creamed butter and sugar. Now deftly and thoroughly fold in the rest of the flour.

Spoon into a buttered pudding basin and cover with a circle of buttered foil that is big enough to give room for the pudding to rise.

Make sure the foil is well sealed round the brim of the basin so that no steam, which would make the top of the pudding wet, can get in. Have the steamer ready on the stove so that it is good and hot, ready to give the mixture its initial 'push into space'!

Steam for 1½ to 1¾ hours. Remember to top up the steamer with boiling water.

When serving, carefully remove the foil, run a knife around the sides of the basin and invert on to a warm serving dish.

Pond pudding

Serves 5 or 6

Suet Crust
8 oz self-raising flour
4 oz suet (or ½ grated butter,
 ½ suet)

¼ pint water
1 tsp grated lemon rind

Filling
4 oz Demerara sugar
2 oz sultanas
2 oz currants

1 large juicy thin-skinned
 lemon
4 oz hard unsalted butter

Dredge flour, suet and lemon rind together. Add water and mix deftly into a soft dough. Well butter a 2½ pint pudding basin. Line with suet crust, reserving approximately one-third of the pastry for the lid.

Prick the lemon all over with a bodkin. Cut the refrigerator-hard butter into small squares. Disperse half of this with half the fruit and sugar into the lined basin. Press the lemon into the centre of this, then pack the remaining ingredients around. The basin should be full.

Wet the pastry edges, fit the lid, sealing well. Cover with buttered foil, making a pleat across the top to allow the crust to rise. Steam for 3 hours.

Pies and pastries

Rich Bakewell pudding

Serves 8

I have called it 'pudding' as this is what I understand the Bakewell-ese do: though I cannot imagine why they haven't either looked up old recipes for this lovely sweet or improved on the ones they already use. I have been to Bakewell many times, and have yet to taste a really good one. So here is my version of this national pie, tart or pudding. It has a really rich pastry – *pâte frollé* or 'finger-tip pastry' we call it.

Pastry case
4 oz plain white flour
3 oz unsalted butter (at room temperature and cut into small bits)

1½ oz ground almonds
1 egg yolk
2 oz castor sugar
⅓ tsp vanilla essence

Filling
8 oz unsalted butter, softened
8 oz castor sugar
4 eggs, beaten
8 oz ground almonds

1 tsp vanilla essence
2 tbsp sieved apricot or raspberry jam

Sieve the flour into a bowl. Break up the ground almonds so that there are no lumps. Stir them into the sieved flour. Turn this out on to a board or work surface. Make a well and put into this the remaining pastry ingredients. Now, 'peck' with your fingertips at the mixture in the well until it starts to come together, then gradually start to 'peck' in bits of the flour and almond mixture until you have a soft mass: if this gets too messy for you, change to a palette knife and cut and 'chop' the mixture until a sandy texture is arrived at. Press the dough together – don't knead it – cover with a clean cloth or put into a plastic bag dredged with plain flour and refrigerate for an hour.

Roll the pastry out and line an 8 inch flan ring or deep pie plate. Fit a foil pad as described on page 148, and bake blind at gas mark 7, 425°F (220°C) for 10 minutes, then gas mark 5, 375°F (190°C) for a further 10 minutes.

Cream together the butter and sugar until almost white and very fluffy. Beat in the eggs and essence. Fold in the ground almonds. Spoon the jam onto the bottom of the pastry shell and spread carefully, then spoon the rest of the filling into the pastry shell. Bake at gas mark 4, 350°F (180°C) for 45–50 minutes.

Serve hot, warm or cold with thick pouring cream or soured cream.

Cambridge tart

Serves 5 or 6

8 oz rich shortcrust pastry (*see* page 155 for method)	3 oz castor sugar
	2 large egg yolks
4 oz marmalade, sieved	
3 oz unsalted butter	

Line an 8 inch flan ring with the pastry (see page 152 for method) and bake blind.

Spread the sieved marmalade over the bottom of the cooked pastry. Cream the butter and sugar in a basin: beat in the egg yolks.

Arrange the basin over a pan of boiling water and stir the mixture until thick: pour over the marmalade and bake at gas mark 3, 325°F (170°C) for 15 minutes.

Serve cold with whipped cream or egg custard.

Chocolate almond tart

Serves 8

Pastry

3 oz unsalted butter	1 egg yolk
5 oz plain flour	2 tbsp cold water
1 oz castor sugar	

Filling

2 oz self-raising flour	Finely grated rind of 1 lemon
2 tbsp cocoa	2 tbsp lemon juice
4 oz unsalted butter	4 heaped tbsp sieved raspberry
4 oz castor sugar	jam
2 medium eggs, lightly beaten	Icing sugar
1 tsp vanilla essence	
5 oz ground almonds, rubbed through a sieve	

Well butter a loose-bottomed 10 inch tart tin or flan ring (the final result should be 2 inches deep). If you are a crinkle dish addict, then this pastry must first be baked blind or you'll have a soggy bottom. Rub the butter into the flour and toss in the sugar. Beat the yolk and water together and add to the mixture using a fork and working everything into a loose dough. Form into a round pad.

Leave to rest for half-an-hour. Roll out evenly and line the tin. Put to rest again.

Sieve the flour and cocoa together. Cream the butter and sugar until light and fluffy. Gradually add the beaten eggs, lemon rind and essence to the butter mixture. Fold in the flour mixture and ground almonds. Mix to a dropping consistence with the lemon juice.

Spread the jam liberally on the base of the pastry shell. Spoon in the mixture and level the top somewhat. Bake at gas mark 7, 425°F (220°C) for 15 minutes, then at gas mark 4, 350°F (180°C) for a further 15 minutes or until cooked.

Serve warm or cold. Dredge the top with icing sugar just before serving.

Walnut 'pye'

Serves 8

This recipe arrived in America around 1776 and was most likely the forerunner of their now famous Pecan pie.

Pastry

6 oz plain white flour	2 oz icing sugar
4 oz unsalted butter	1 egg
1 tsp lemon juice	1 tbsp cold water

Filling

4 oz ground almonds	1 tbsp lemon juice
4 oz castor sugar	1 tbsp honey
2 eggs	Icing supar
4 oz walnuts roughly chopped	

Rub the butter into the flour until you have a sandy texture; sift in the sugar; beat egg, water and lemon juice together, make a well in the pastry mix and add this, forming deftly into a dough. Leave to rest for half an hour. Roll out two-thirds of the pastry and line a flan ring or pie dish, retaining the other third for a lid.

Separate the eggs; cream the yolks with the sugar and honey until white and fluffy. Stir in the ground almonds and lemon juice; add the chopped walnuts. Stiffly beat the whites and fold into the nutty mixture.

Fill the flan or pie shell, wet the edges and fit the lid, seal and fork round the edges. Bake in the centre of a pre-heated oven at gas mark 6, 400°F (200°C) for 40 minutes.

Cool, dredge with icing sugar before serving with plenty of unsweetened whipped cream.

The pie is extra rich when the filling is made with 4 oz dark brown sugar in place of the castor sugar.

Southern pecan pie

Serves 8 to 10

Pastry

2 oz unsalted butter	1 egg yolk
2 oz lard	1 tbsp lemon juice
2 oz flour	1 tbsp water
1 tsp icing sugar	

Filling

3 eggs	6 oz castor sugar
12 oz maple syrup, light clear honey, or ordinary syrup	4 oz melted butter
½ tsp salt	8 oz (shelled weight) pecans (or walnuts)
2 tsp vanilla extract	

Make the pastry first: rub fats into flour, sift in sugar, beat the egg yolk with the lemon juice and water and add to the mixture, mixing to soft dough.

Line a 9 inch loose-bottomed pie tin (1 to 1½ inches deep) and chill well.

Next, make the filling: beat the eggs, beat in rest of the ingredients, fold in pecans and turn into pastry shell. Bake at gas mark 6, 400°F (200°C) for 40 minutes or until set.

Serve warm or cold with vanilla ice-cream.

If you have difficulty obtaining pecans, use walnuts instead – it's equally delicious.

Royal 'pyes'

Serves 8

Pastry

8 oz plain flour	1 egg yolk
5 oz butter	3 tbsp water
2 oz sugar	

Topping

2 egg whites	4 oz castor sugar

Filling

8 oz good mincemeat	¾ oz unsalted butter
2 egg yolks	1 tbsp rum (optional)
Rind and juice of 1 lemon	

Make up pastry in the usual way. Cream thoroughly butter, yolks, lemon rind and juice and rum: combine well with mincemeat. Line tart tins or pie plate with thinly rolled pastry. Three-quarters fill with the mincemeat mixture. Bake at gas mark 5, 375°F (190°C) for 30 minutes.

Whisk the egg whites until they stand in peaks. Add the sugar a tablespoon at a time and beat until the meringue is stiff.

Top tarts with meringue (using a piping bag). Bake for further 30 minutes at gas mark 2, 300°F (150°C), until meringue is crisp. Serve warm or cold.

Chocolate 'pye'

Serves 8

Pastry

8 oz plain flour
5 oz butter
2 oz sugar

1 egg yolk
3 tbsp water

Filling

10 oz dark chocolate
5 eggs, separated
2 level tsp gelatine crystals
2 tbsp cold water

4 tbsp sherry or rum
1 tsp vanilla essence
see Method

Garnish

Whipped cream
Toasted walnuts or
  flakes of chocolate

Make up the pastry in the usual way. Line a 9 inch flan ring and bake blind. Allow to cool.

In a round bottomed bowl put the chocolate, broken into bits, and sherry or rum made up to ¼ pint with cold water. (If sherry is used add 1 tsp vanilla essence.) Set the bowl over a pan of boiling water and allow to melt and get quite hot. Stir in the gelatine softened in the cold water, making sure it is totally dissolved in the chocolate mixture. Remove the bowl from the heat and beat in the egg yolks one by one. Leave to cool but not set. Stiffly beat the whites and cut and fold these thoroughly into the chocolate mixture. Fill into the pastry case and put to set, but do not refrigerate (this will make the pastry go soggy).

Decorate with a border of whipped cream, sprinkled with toasted walnuts or flakes of chocolate.

Tarte aux pommes Strasbourgeoise
(Strasbourg apple custard tart)

Serves 5 or 6

Pastry (see page 155)
1 lb cooking apples
3 oz castor sugar
¼ pint cream

1 scant oz flour
½ tsp vanilla essence
Lemon juice

Line a 9 inch flan ring with the pastry. Line the pastry with buttered foil (butter-side down) and fill with dried beans or small pebbles, to keep the pastry from falling in. Bake blind at gas mark 7, 425°F (220°C), for 15 minutes. Leave to cool somewhat, then carefully remove the foil.

Meanwhile peel, core and quarter the apples putting them into acidulated water. Mix the sugar and flour together and gradually add the cream and essence. Drain and dry the apples with paper towels.

Now cut each quarter apple into 3 half-moons. Arrange in overlapping concentric circles on the base of the pastry shell (leave the flan ring on). Return the tart to the oven at gas mark 6, 400°F (200°C), for 10 to 15 minutes, until the apples just begin to 'give'.

Reduce the temperature to gas mark 4, 350°F (180°C).

Pour over the cream mixture and bake for a further 15 to 20 minutes until pastry is crisp, apples cooked and cream mixture set.

Shoofly pie

Serves 5 or 6

Whether Shoofly pie is from the stoves of the coloured cooks in America's Deep South, where it is said flies descended on this sweet sticky pie as it was cooking and had to be shoo-ed away, or from the Pennsylvanian Dutch is open to conjecture but, wherever it originated, it's very good.

Filling
4 oz muscatel raisins
2 oz soft brown sugar
¼ tsp bicarbonate of soda

4 dsp rum, whisky or water

Pastry

4 oz plain flour	1 egg yolk (small)
2 oz unsalted butter	2 tbsp cold water
1 oz castor sugar	

Topping

4 oz plain white flour	¼ tsp nutmeg
½ tsp cinnamon	2 oz butter
¼ tsp ground ginger	2 oz brown sugar

Soak the first four ingredients overnight to plump up the fruit.

Next day, make pastry in usual way and line a 7 inch loose-bottomed tin.

Make the topping by sieving the flour and spices. Rub in the butter to a crumb-like consistency.

Spoon the soaked raisins into the pastry case. Spread over the crumb mixture. Sprinkle the sugar on top.

Bake at gas mark 7, 425°F (220°C) for 15 minutes, then lower to gas mark 5, 375°F (190°C) for 20 minutes.

Serve warm or cold with thick cream, sour cream or ice-cream.

Clafoutis aux cerises (Cherry maraschino flan)

Serves 5 or 6

Pastry

6 oz plain white flour	2 oz butter
2 oz lard	Water to mix

Filling

12 oz pitted black cherries	1 oz sugar
Sieved cherry jam	2 oz self-raising flour
1 egg	2 tbsp Maraschino (or one
1 oz unsalted butter	miniature bottle)

Whipped cream

Make up the pastry in the usual way. (For richer version use the recipe on page 155.)

Line an 8 inch flan ring with this and spread with a layer of the sieved jam. Arrange the pitted cherries evenly over the jam. Make the topping as follows: cream the butter and sugar, beat in the egg and Maraschino, fold in the flour and spread over the cherries.

Bake in a pre-heated oven at gas mark 5, 375°F (190°C) for 35–40 minutes. Serve hot or cold with whipped cream.

(I usually bake the pastry case blind for 15–20 minutes as I like my pastry particularly well baked. Other fruit can be used for this dish.)

Tarte tatin (Caramel upside down apple pie)

Serves 6

Filling

4 oz unsalted butter (Dutch or French softened)
6 oz castor sugar

5 large dessert apples
Squeeze of lemon

Pastry

6 oz self-raising flour
4 oz unsalted butter
2 tsp icing sugar

Pinch of salt
1 egg beaten with 1 tbsp cold water

Make up the pastry and leave in a cool place to rest for half an hour. Then roll out all the pastry to make just a lid to fit your tin.

Use a metal seamless tin (about 10 inch long). Peel, core and slice the apples into water to which you have added a squeeze of lemon juice to prevent discolouration. Place a cushion of the softened butter over the entire base of the tin. Cover with a layer of sugar, using it all.

Drain and pat dry the apples and arrange these over the butter and sugar.

Cover with 'lid' of pastry as you would do for an ordinary pie but omitting the pastry edges.

Bake in a pre-heated oven gas mark 7, 425°F (220°C) for 45 minutes.

If, after 20 minutes, the pastry is burning, lower the temperature a notch, but remember the pastry ought to be very brown and crisp. Place a serving dish over the finished *Tarte* and invert the two.

The finished result should be a sticky caramel apple mixture on top of the crisp pastry.

Serve with chilled cream or sour cream.

(If you have a thin-bottomed tin and an Aga, success should be immediate. If not, you may, after having made the *Tarte* once and having perhaps discovered that the marriage of your particular mould and your particular oven doesn't produce a rich dark sticky caramel, have to make a fudge with the butter and sugar in a pan on top of the stove, taking the mixture to almost caramel stage before pouring into your tin and topping with the sliced apples and pastry lid.)

Maids of Honour

Pastry

8 oz plain flour	1 egg yolk
5 oz unsalted butter	3 tbsp cold water
2 tsp icing sugar	

Filling

3 oz castor sugar	Rind of 1 lemon, shredded
2 egg yolks	4 oz ground almonds
2 oz unsalted butter	Quince jelly or conserve
1 heaped tsp self-raising flour	(or raspberry jam)
3 tbsp thick cream	Icing sugar

First make the pastry. Sieve the sugar and flour together; cut the butter into small pieces and lightly rub into the flour. Make a well in this sandy-textured mixture, add the egg yolk and water all at once, and form quickly and deftly into a soft dough. Leave this to rest for 30 minutes before rolling out and lining either one large flan ring or smaller deep tartlet tins.

Now make the filling. Cream the butter and sugar thoroughly. Beat in the small quantity of flour. Beat in the egg yolks. Stir in the ground almonds and lemon rind, incorporating them completely. Finally, 'slacken' the mixture with the cream.

Whether you are making one large tart or individual ones, it is better that they should be deep enough to hold plenty of filling. Put a teaspoon of quince jelly or conserve into each tart case, spread this over the bottom and put a good measure of the almond mixture on top.

Bake in the centre of the oven at gas mark 6, 400°F (200°C), for 20 minutes (a larger tart will take up to 30 minutes). Put onto a cooling tray; dust with icing sugar before serving either warm or cold.

Creamy desserts

Caramel cream with rum-baked pears

Serves 6

For the caramel

3 oz castor sugar

A little water

¼ tsp cream of tartar

For the custard

2 oz castor sugar

5 eggs

½ pint milk

½ pint single cream

Vanilla pod or ½ tsp vanilla
  essence

For the garnish

2 oz unsalted butter

6 pear halves

3 oz sugar

Large glass Jamaica rum
  (optional)

Make the caramel first, to coat a 1½ pint mould. Put the sugar in a pan with a little water and the cream of tartar. Bring to the boil, stirring until the sugar is dissolved evenly. Then don't stir again, or crystals will form. Leave the sugar to caramelise slowly: it should be darker than golden syrup.

Have a sink of cold water ready to plunge the bottom of the pan into as soon as you think it is a good caramel. Pour into the mould and swirl around until the mould is completely coated. Obviously, you will need to use oven gloves or two folded cloths for this, as it is hot work!

Now make the custard. Preheat the oven to gas mark 3, 325°F (170°C). Have a bain-marie of hot water at the ready (a roasting tin half-filled with hot water will do). Cream the sugar and eggs. Infuse the milk, cream and vanilla, slowly letting it come to the boil. Pour it over the egg mixture, stirring well. Strain the custard into the waiting caramel-lined mould. Place this in the bain-marie and bake in the oven for about 45 minutes, or until the custard is set.

While the caramel cream is cooking, prepare the garnish. Melt the butter and fry the pear halves until brown. Remove them from the pan, add the sugar and cook until dissolved. Add the rum – having lowered the heat in case the alcohol ignites – and simmer this syrup until thick and viscous. Pour over the waiting pear halves, and put to chill.

When the caramel cream is cooked, leave to cool, then chill. Unmould the cream, and arrange the pear halves round the edges of the dish. Serve the extra 'sauce' separately, or pour round the dish all at one time. Extra whipped cream can be served if liked.

Sillabub

Serves 6 or 8

The name for this Tudor confection comes from the French town of Sille where champagne (originally used in the making of this 'drink') was made.

1 pint double cream
¼ pint Madeira
1 level tsp cinnamon

Juice and rind of 1 lemon and orange
3 oz castor sugar

Half whip the cream. Add the rest of the ingredients and continue beating until the mixture just stands in peaks. Fill individual glasses and chill well.

Red fruit brûlée

Serves 6 to 8

8 oz punnet redcurrants
8 oz fresh raspberries
8 oz strawberries, cut into quarters
2 tbsp liqueur, such as Orange Curaçao, Grand Marnier, Drambuie (optional)
Castor sugar for dredging fruit and topping

2 whole eggs
6 egg yolks
2 oz castor sugar (or less)
1 tsp cornflour
1 pint single cream
Vanilla pod or 1 tsp vanilla essence

Clean the fruit, sprinkle with the liqueur, dredge with a tablespoon of sugar, cover with plastic film and chill for two hours or more.

Meanwhile, cream the whole eggs, the yolks, 2 oz sugar and cornflour in a heatproof bowl. Bring the cream to the boil with the vanilla, pour over the egg mixture whisking well all the time.

The cream should thicken, but this depends on many factors, so if it doesn't, arrange the bowl over a pan of boiling water and whisk slowly but thoroughly until it does. Stand the bowl immediately in a sink of cold water and continue whisking until the residual heat has gone. Leave to cool completely.

Put the chilled fruits in the bottom of a 3 inch deep 2 to 2½ pint flameproof dish. Pour the thickened cream over this. Dredge the top with enough castor sugar to give about an eighth-inch layer. Brown under a preheated hot grill. Cool and serve cold. If you refrigerate it the topping will soften.

Burn't creams
Serves 6 or 8

If you are one of the innocents who fondly imagines this recipe is from the stoves of France, forget it. Trinity College, Cambridge, has a better claim to the original than anywhere across the Channel!

8 egg yolks	½ vanilla pod, or the grated
1 pint double cream	rind of ½ lemon or 1 tsp
1 tsp cornflour	vanilla essence
2 oz castor sugar	Extra castor sugar

When dealing with anything where egg yolks are the thickening agent, it is wise to have a bowl of cold water at the ready into which you can plunge the receptacle in which you have thickened the cream; this will remove any residual heat which may be strong enough to curdle the mixture.

Cream together the yolks, sugar and cornflour in a bowl. Slowly bring to the boil the pint of cream with whichever flavour you choose to use, giving time for the flavour to infuse. Strain onto the yolk mixture. Arrange the bowl over a pan of boiling water and stir the cream continuously until it is quite thick and the whisk leaves a very definite trail.

Pour into a shallow single dish or individual pots. Put to cool, then chill in the refrigerator. Just before serving, stand the creams in a tin of cold water which will fit comfortably under the grill. Pre-heat the grill, dredge the top of the cream with castor sugar and let the sugar caramelise.

Do not put the creams back into the refrigerator as this will soften the glass-like finish you have just created with the sugar.

Old English sherry trifle

Serves 8 or 10

Custard sauce (page 138)

Base
2 × 7 inch fatless sponge
  cakes or 1 packet small
  sponge cakes

1 lb apricot purée, apricot jam,
  or quince jelly
¼ bottle medium dry sherry

Topping
1 pint double cream
4 oz glacé cherries
4 oz blanched or toasted
  almonds
2 oz each crystallised apricots,
  crystallised pears or
  Carlsbad plums

2 oz crystallised chestnuts
4 oz ratafia biscuits
Angelica

Use good quality sponge cakes. First make up the Custard. Split the sponge cakes in half across their middles: liberally spread them with purée, jam or jelly, sandwich them together and cut into 1 inch fingers. Arrange these in a shallow trifle dish, about 12 inches across the top and about 3 inches deep.

Sprinkle the sponge fingers with plenty of sherry and pour the waiting custard over them. Cool the trifle base completely. (If the bowl is glass, wipe away any condensation from the sides, as this will look unsightly when the trifle is cold.)

Prepare all the topping ingredients – the actual quantities will depend on the area of trifle to be covered and this is bound to vary slightly.

Cut the crystallised apricots or pears and chestnuts and Carlsbad plums into attractive quarters. Cut long spikes of angelica. Empty the packet of ratafias to free them from biscuit crumbs. Make sure that the blanched or toasted almonds are cold or they will melt the cream. Put each topping ready on a separate plate.

Whip the cream until it just stands in peaks but doesn't look as though it will be cheese at any minute! Spread a thick layer over the trifle. Decorate at will with the other topping ingredients.

You may like to make a fresh fruit trifle and in this case use fresh fruits only for decoration and stick them into the bed of whipped cream at the last moment so that the juices do not draw and spoil the look of the trifle. A purée of fruit can replace the jam in the sponge cakes. Particularly suitable fruits to use are strawberries or raspberries and fresh apricots. If you are using raspberries use Kirsch instead of sherry.

Butter'd orange

Serves 6

This is the recipe which first convinced me that there were delicate and fine dishes in the English repertory.

2 large juicy oranges
2 oz castor sugar
5 large egg yolks
1 tbsp rose-water
4 oz unsalted butter

¼ pint double cream
½ a candied orange or 1 tbsp very finely chopped candied orange peel
1 tsp grated orange rind

Grate just the oily orange zest from one of the oranges. Squeeze the two oranges and strain the juice into a bowl which will fit over a pan of boiling water. Add the egg yolks, sugar, rose-water and grated rind. Mix well together and then whisk gently over the boiling water until the mixture is thick and ribbons. Remove from heat.

Cut the butter into inch pieces, let it soften at room temperature then squeeze this through the fingers into the thickened mixture, beating well as you go along. Shred the candied orange on a grater so that it is as fine as you can manage, fold this into the mixture and finally fold in the half-whipped cream.

Pour into individual glasses or pots and put in the refrigerator to set. Decorate at will with whipped cream and crystallised rose petals or flaked almonds.

Coque au lait (French baked custard pudding)

Serves 4

1 pint milk
¼ pint single cream
3 egg yolks

3 whole eggs
2 oz castor sugar
2 tbsp brandy or Armagnac

Butter a china ovenproof dish with unsalted butter. Cream whole eggs, yolks and sugar. Add brandy. Bring milk and cream to the boil and pour over beaten eggs whisking all the time. Strain into china dish.

Stand the dish in a second container of hot water. Bake at gas mark 4, 350°F (180°C) for 35 to 40 minutes or until set. Cool, chill and serve.

Sabayon au rhum (Rum custard)

Serves 6

¾ pint sweet white wine
¼ pint Jamaican rum
Juice of half lemon

Strips of rind of half a lemon
4 oz castor sugar
8 egg yolks

Select a stainless steel or Pyrex bowl which will sit comfortably over a pan of boiling water – the base of the bowl must be in contact with the water underneath.

Mix all the ingredients together, having first creamed the yolks and sugar until almost white.

Set the basin over the boiling water and, using a balloon whisk, stir *continuously* until the custard is thick. It can take up to 20 minutes to thicken, so be patient. The whisk should leave a definite trail.

Pour into individual glasses and serve either hot (very good) or cold (not quite so good).

Serve with boudoir biscuits or petticoat tail shortbreads.

Vanilla Bavarian cream

Serves 8

1 pint milk
1 vanilla pod or a little vanilla
  essence
8 egg yolks
8 oz sugar

4 level tsp powdered gelatine
A little cold water
1 pint cream
Fresh raspberries

Bring milk to the boil with vanilla pod or vanilla essence. Whip the yolks and sugar to a light creamy texture. Add the milk. Stir the milk, egg yolks and sugar mixture over a low heat until just under the boil, until coating the back of a wooden spoon, test by drawing your finger across it and seeing that the mixture leaves a trail.

Place 2 tablespoons of cold water in a pan, add gelatine and stir over a low heat until transparent. *Do not boil*. Add to mixture, stirring in very thoroughly. Place in refrigerator. When cool and on the point of setting, whisk cream to the same consistency and fold in. Pour in individual pots and allow to set.

Serve topped with fresh raspberries.

This recipe can be varied by selecting different flavourings such as rum, coffee, and Grand Marnier.

Old English baked rice pudding

Serves 5 to 6

I wonder how many realise what an elaborate confection a rice pudding used to be. It is certainly a far cry from the rather wet milk and rice product often served today. The Georgians would have put a rim of prettily decorated puff pastry round the edge of the dish, though this ought to be baked first in a hot oven should you think of embarking on such an elaboration.

4 oz pudding rice	2 oz muscatel raisins
Rind of 1 lemon	2 oz sultanas
1 pint milk	1 oz chopped peel or glacé
2 oz castor sugar	cherries
4 eggs	1 sherry glass of brandy
2 oz unsalted butter	Grated nutmeg

In a large pan, bring plenty of water to the boil. Wash the rice, put this into the water and boil for 17 minutes exactly. Rinse the rice in a sieve under cold running water.

In a double boiler, infuse the lemon rind with the milk and sugar. Beat the eggs in a separate basin. Whisk in the hot milk and return the mixture to the pan, stirring all the time until the sauce coats the back of a spoon.

Take the pan away from the heat (off the water, that is), add the butter, fruits, brandy and cold rice. Butter an ovenproof dish and pour the mixture into this.

Stand the dish in a second dish or meat tin containing hot water. Grate a little nutmeg over the top and bake the pudding at gas mark 2, 300°F (150°C) for half an hour, or until the pudding is set but not split.

Serve with pouring cream.

Walnut charlotte

Serves 10 or 12

1 lb unsalted butter
10 egg yolks
10 oz sieved icing sugar
10 oz walnuts pulverised in a
blender or food processor

Langue de chat biscuits
(flat sponge fingers)
Extra walnut halves
Whipped cream to decorate

Cream the butter well. Add the lightly-beaten egg yolks and cream together again. Add the sieved icing sugar. Blend in the walnuts.

Turn into a cake tin with a removable base, the sides lined with the *langue de chat* biscuits, and chill.

When quite set, lift out and cover the top with whipped cream and decorate with walnut halves.

This is a very rich pudding, halve the quantities for a party of only five or six. This sweet is ideal for a special party. I make mine in a long tin and cut portions about half-an-inch thick. A round tin can be used but care must be taken not to cut thick slices.

Roman cheesecake

Serves 8 or 10

This delicious sweet is easy to make.

For the cake
2 oz unsalted butter
8 oz castor sugar
1 lb cream cheese
2 tbsp any good flavoured
honey

4 fl oz single cream
1 tsp vanilla essence
5 eggs, separated
2 oz plain flour, sifted
4 oz flaked almonds

For the topping
2 oz soft brown sugar
1 tsp cinnamon

2 oz flaked almonds
Sieved icing sugar

Cream the butter and castor sugar until light and fluffy. Add the cheese and beat well. Add the honey, cream, vanilla essence, egg yolks and flour. Mix well. Lightly fold in the stiffly beaten egg whites together with the flaked almonds.

Pour into a well-buttered spring form tin and sprinkle evenly with the topping ingredients. (It is not necessary to line the spring form with short crust pastry for this recipe, but it is an option.) Bake for 1 hour at gas mark 3, 325°F (170°C). Then turn off the heat and allow to cool *in the oven* to prevent a rift from forming.

Dredge with sieved icing sugar before serving.

Chocolate trifle
Serves 12 (8 inch diameter, 4 inch deep bowl)

Many folk make this trifle with all chocolate things such as chocolate sponge and chocolate buttercream inside the sponge as well . . . this I find too much as it actually kills the flavour of the chocolate. I don't even sweeten the cream, as I like the foil of the clean unsweetened cream against the richest of chocolate sauces and the slight tanginess of the jam (try using a plain fruit purée, remembering that apricots and raspberries are excellent with chocolate). Here I have used pears. I think you'll enjoy this. I have also added a few bitter chocolate coated almonds to the top (these you can buy at any good confectioners).

For the trifle base
2 packets commercial trifle
   sponges
12 oz apricot jam (low sugar)
1 pint double cream
Liqueur (optional)

6 small pears, peeled, cored, cut in half and poached in a light syrup, cooled and drained
Ratafias

Chocolate sauce
3 tbsp Jamaican or Demerara
   rum
3 tbsp water
3 oz of a good dark chocolate
5 egg yolks

1 oz castor sugar mixed with 2 heaped dsp cocoa
3/4 pint single cream
1 tsp vanilla essence

For the decoration
Ratafias
Chocolate squares, flakes or
   buttons
Bitter chocolate coated
   almonds

Crystallised fruits (optional)
Liqueur (optional)

Make the chocolate sauce first. In a basin over hot water, melt the chocolate with the rum and water. In another basin cream the egg yolks, adding the cocoa and sugar mixture. Beat until fluffy. Bring the cream to the boil with the vanilla essence. Pour over the egg mixture whisking all the time.

Incorporate thoroughly. Then pour on to the chocolate mixture, incorporating this thoroughly too. Leave to cool, but not chill.

Next, assemble the trifle. Split the sponges in half and spread *liberally* with a low-sugar apricot jam. Cut into pieces diagonally.

Half whip the cream. Arrange the trifle sponges, pears and the odd ratafia biscuit in a glass bowl, spooning over half of the cream and all of the chocolate sauce as you go along.

Whip the remaining cream until it stands in stiff peaks. Fill into a piping bag fitted with a star tube, and decorate the top of the trifle at will with swirls of cream, ratafias, crystallised fruits, chocolate squares, buttons or flakes and the chocolate coated almonds. Just how rich you make this is up to you and will depend on your eye (and the state of the housekeeping), but a trifle should be rich and the opposite to what the name implies!

For very special occasions, I dribble some appropriate liqueur over the sponges and add a drop or two to the cream as I whip it. Poire Guillaume – Pear William – is excellent for this as it is dry in flavour and adds a marvellously unexpected contrast to the rich trifle.

Quince creams
Serves 6

If you are in an area where quinces are not readily available then select good-flavoured pears instead, and add a heaped tablespoon of quince jelly which is sold in most good groceries and supermarkets.

1 lb quinces or pears
2 oz castor sugar
½ pint double cream
3 egg yolks
2 oz unsalted butter

1 tbsp quince jelly
¼ tsp powdered mace or cinnamon
Extra cream for decorating (optional)

Wash the fruit but do not peel it, just quarter and core it. Cut

171

into rough, though even-sized, pieces. Put into a pan with the butter, sugar, jelly and spice. Add a couple of tablespoons of cold water and slowly stew the fruit over a very low heat until it is quite pulped. Press the pulp through a sieve (or do this on a blender). Beat in the yolks whilst the pulp is still hot. Allow to cool, then add the half whipped cream, incorporating thoroughly.

Chill before serving, decorating with swirls of whipped cream if liked.

Edwardian charlotte

Serves 6 or 8

12 oz apricots (stewed or tinned)	1 tsp vanilla essence
¼ pint of the juice	2 tbsp Amaretto liqueur (or Kirsch)
1 oz castor sugar	½ pint whipping cream
½ oz gelatine	Boudoir biscuits
Beaten egg white	Decoration *see* Method

Cut a circle of greaseproof paper to fit the bottom of a mould. Line the mould with Boudoir biscuits, dipping the edges into a little beaten egg white to help them stick – flat side face inwards.

Bring juice to boil. Dissolve sugar and gelatine in this. Allow to cool somewhat and add the liqueur and essence, then blend this with the apricots as fine as possible (or laboriously press through a hair-sieve). Half whip the cream and fold into the fruit purée. Pour into the lined mould and put to set.

Turn out and decorate the top at will with angelica, blanched almonds and crystallised apricots – a cheaper decoration is to use only ratafia biscuits.

Mousses and soufflés

Cold tangerine soufflé
Serves 8 to 10

If you mould the soufflé, do not remove the paper collar until half an hour before serving, as it is very light-textured and may well collapse – which in no way impairs its quality: in fact it is an indication of its lightness. To eliminate this does entail using more gelatine, which in turn would produce a firmer texture – edible indeed but not so attractive to the palate.

10 tangerines
Juice of 2 lemons
1 heaped dsp gelatine crystals
10 eggs, separated
4 oz castor sugar

½ tsp cochineal or edible red food dye
½ pint double or whipping cream

Prepare a 2½ pint soufflé dish with a paper collar before starting to make the soufflé.

Lightly grate the orange part of the rind from 5 of the tangerines. Squeeze the juice from all 10, plus the juice of the lemons. This should make ¾ pint.

Dissolve the gelatine in 2 tablespoons boiling water in a cup.

Put the egg yolks into a round-bottomed bowl together with the sugar, juice and rind. Arrange the bowl over a pan of boiling water. Make sure the water is in contact with the bottom of the bowl. Whisk until it is thick and the whisk leaves a distinct trail. During the whisking incorporate the gelatine.

Now stand the bowl in a sink of cold water, stirring from time to time to ensure even cooling. Add the cochineal to the cream and half whip it until the whisk leaves a distinct trail. Beat the egg whites until they stand up in stiff peaks.

When the mousse mixture is cool but not setting, quickly fold in the cream and finally the stiffly beaten whites, I always add the first third of the whites and work them well into the mixture to slacken it so that I can work swiftly and lightly with the remainder.

Fill your prepared dish with the mousse mixture. Let it set in a cool pantry or the bottom of your refrigerator.

Serve with double cream or dress it up with whipped cream, but *don't* use tinned mandarin segments as these make the cream run and interfere with the subtle flavour of this mousse.

Chocolate, ginger and orange mousse

Serves 8

8 oz dark chocolate broken
   into bits (Menier, Terry's
   Bitter or Cadbury's
   Bournville)
2 oz unsalted butter
Finely grated rind of half and
   the juice of one orange

¼ tsp ground ginger
1 level tsp gelatine crystals
4 large eggs, separated
2 large pieces stem ginger
   finely shredded or chopped
Chilled cream

Arrange a basin over a pan of boiling water. Put in the chocolate, butter, juice and ground ginger: leave to soften and get quite hot, stirring occasionally.

Sprinkle the gelatine crystals on to the mixture and stir in well, ensuring that they dissolve. Remove the basin from the heat and beat in the egg yolks one at a time. Leave to cool in a sink of cold water, stirring from time to time. Add the stem ginger.

Beat the egg whites until they stand in stiff peaks. Beat a third of them well into the cooled chocolate mixture: cut and fold in the remainder with a slotted spoon, incorporating lightly but thoroughly. Pour into 8 individual glasses, cover with plastic film and put to set in the refrigerator.

Serve with a little chilled cream poured over the surface.

Cream cheese mousse with Drambuie

Serves 4 to 6

4 eggs, separated
3 oz castor sugar
6 oz cream cheese (e.g. Petit
   Suisse)

¼ pint double cream
3 tbsp Drambuie

Cream the yolks and sugar until light and fluffy. Using a balloon whisk gradually incorporate the cream cheese. Whip the cream with the Drambuie until it stands in soft but definite peaks; stir into the mixture. Beat the egg whites until they stand in stiff peaks, cut and fold these into the mixture.

Chill well overnight in a plastic container in the freezer compartment of the refrigerator. Spoon into tall glasses.

Serve with a Fresh Raspberry sauce (see page 135).

Chocolate dacquoise
Serves 8

This sweet is made in two parts: the meringue cakes and mousse mixture are made a day ahead, and the Dacquoise assembled with its topping only on the day it is to be eaten.

Nut meringue cakes

8 egg whites
12 oz castor sugar
1 tsp vanilla essence

6 oz hazelnuts
1 tbsp cornflour, sieved

Well butter two baking sheets and line with silicone paper. Draw three oblongs, 10 × 4½ inches, on each sheet. Whip the egg whites to soft peaks, adding a quarter of the sugar as you do so. Continue whipping until the whites stand in stiff peaks: during the last few movements add the vanilla and the remaining sugar. Fold in gradually, carefully but thoroughly, the crushed nuts and cornflour. Divide this meringue mixture between the six oblongs, spreading with a palette knife to the edges drawn, and levelling them somewhat.

Bake at gas mark 2, 300°F (150°C) for an hour or until pale-brown and crisp. Cool a little, then remove paper and place meringues on wire cooling tray to cool completely. They can be frozen or stored in an airtight tin, and so can be made well in advance.

Mousse mixture

12 oz Bournville chocolate,
    broken into smallish pieces
6 egg whites

1 pint double cream
1 tsp vanilla essence

Melt the chocolate in a large (6 pint) basin set over simmering water. Leave to cool but *not* set. Meanwhile, whisk egg whites to stiff peaks, and the cream to soft peaks; add vanilla essence to cream.

Stir in one-third of the egg whites well. *Fold* in with a slotted spoon or wire balloon the whisked cream and finally the remaining egg whites. Clean the edges of the bowl, cover with plastic film, and store overnight in the fridge.

Assemble the Dacquoise on the morning of the day on which it is required; neatly trim four of the oblong meringue cakes. Arrange one of these on a wire cooling rack set over a baking tray or you can stand the Dacquoise on a piece of foil the same width but four inches larger at each end to ease the lifting – you just gently pull the foil from under it once it is transferred. Mentally divide the mousse into four parts. Using a palette knife, spread the cake with a good ½ inch layer of the chocolate mousse. Arrange the second and third meringue cakes on top, spreading them with the mousse in a similar fashion. Invert and fit the top meringue and leave plain. (The inverted side will be flat.) Using the remaining mousse mixture, coat the sides and ends, smoothing them over.

Chill the Dacquoise for 2 hours. Put the remaining two meringue cakes through the fine blade of a Mouli or food processor, to give a fine even crumb mixture. Put into a clean dry bowl and reserve for topping.

Topping

8 oz Bournville chocolate
½ pint double cream

1 tbsp of Kirsch or Pear William (rum or brandy will do)

In a basin, over simmering water, stir the above ingredients until melted and smooth. Leave to cool but not set. Pour down the length of the top of the Dacquoise. Spread evenly over the top, then spread any spillage over the sides.

Press the meringue crumbs on to sides and ends. Put to chill again for an hour or more.

Transfer to a long or oval flat meat dish or cake tray using two spatulas or two fish slices. For ease of serving, cut with a hot knife (dipped into a deep jug of water between each cut).

Chocolate soufflé

Serves 4

3 oz dark chocolate
¼ pint milk
2 oz castor sugar
3 egg yolks
4 egg whites, stiffly beaten

1 tsp vanilla essence
1 level tbsp cornflour
2 tbsp thick cream
Icing sugar

Cream together yolks, sugar, essence, cornflour and cream. In a heavy bottomed pan melt the chocolate in the milk over a low heat, stirring from time to time. Combine the two mixtures in the pan and, stirring all the time, slowly bring to the boil; let the heat go from this before folding in 2 tablespoons of the beaten egg whites and incorporating these well. Deftly fold in the remainder of the egg whites and pour the mixture into a buttered soufflé dish.

Stand the dish on a hot metal tray in a pre-heated oven, gas mark 4, 350°F (180°C). Bake for 45–50 minutes. Dredge the top with icing sugar before serving. Serve either with Hot chocolate sauce (page 137) and/or whipped unsweetened cream.

Gâteaux

Whisky-glazed orange cake

Serves 6 to 8

This way of making orange cake removes this favourite from the tea-table and puts it firmly on the supper or dinner table. Try making it in a well-buttered shaped mould.

The cake
2 eggs, beaten
4 oz unsalted butter
4 oz castor sugar
6 oz self-raising flour plus 1 tsp baking powder, and a pinch of salt sifted together

Finely-grated rind of 1 large orange
Up to ½ pint orange juice to mix

The glaze
4 oz unsalted butter
2 oz castor sugar

2 large tots whisky or rum

Cream butter and sugar together with the grated rind until light and fluffy. Add the beaten eggs gradually adding a modicum of flour if they appear to be splitting (usually due to the temperature being too cold). Mix in the flour, adding orange juice as you go along until you have a soft dropping consistency. Spoon or pour into a well-buttered cake tin.

Bake at gas mark 4, 350°F (180°C) for 45 minutes to 1 hour, or until the cake is resistant to your finger when lightly pressed at its thickest part. Turn out on to a shallow serving dish, prick holes in it with a skewer.

Melt the ingredients for the glaze together in a small pan and spoon over the cake.

Serve warm or cold with whipped cream or soured cream, or even yoghurt.

Brandy Snaps

Serves 6

4 oz plain flour
4 oz butter
4 oz sugar
4 oz golden syrup

¼ oz ground ginger
Juice of half a lemon
Lemon-flavoured whipped cream

Melt sugar, butter and syrup, add the warmed flour, ginger and lemon. Stir well and put out on a well-greased baking-sheet in teaspoonfuls, 6 inches apart.

Bake at gas mark 3, 325°F (170°C) for 10 minutes until golden brown, leave for a few moments to cool, then roll up over the thick handle of a wooden spoon and fill with whipped cream.

Walnut meringue cake with apricots

Serves 8

A meringue-type cake or sweet is a must for all party giving and is almost a bonus, as so often there are egg whites to be used up, particularly in households where mayonnaise-making is prevalent. This handsome cake is ideal for Sunday lunch or as one of your best sweets when party-giving.

5 large egg whites
10 oz castor sugar
6 oz walnuts, crushed
12 oz tin apricot halves,
  drained (or fresh apricots
  macerated in a little liqueur)

½ pint double cream whipped
  to soft peak
Icing sugar for dredging

Line two 8 inch Victoria sandwich tins with silicone paper.

Beat the egg whites, adding half the sugar as you go along and the remainder folded well in at the end of the whisking. The mixture should stand up in peaks.

Fold in the crushed nuts with a slotted spoon. Spoon this mixture equally into the two tins. Bake at gas mark 5, 375°F (190°C) for 35 to 45 minutes. The 'cakes' should be crisp on the outside but a modicum of soft is desirable in the centre.

Turn out carefully on to a wire tray and remove the silicone papers. Return the cakes to the oven with the heat switched off to dry the bases if they appear wet. Leave to cool completely.

Stand the first cake on a piece of greaseproof paper, crust or top side up. Cover with the apricots. Pipe over the whipped cream. Arrange the second cake crusty side uppermost: dredge liberally with sieved icing sugar. Slide the cake on to a serving platter: a large palette knife or fish slice will help here as the cake ought to be very fragile – difficult to cut but scrumptious to eat.

Chestnut, cream cheese and vanilla roll

Serves 5 or 6

An ideal after dinner sweet for a special dinner party.

For the sponge

3 eggs

3 oz castor sugar

1 tsp vanilla essence (where vanilla sugar isn't used)

1 scant oz unsalted butter, melted but cool

3 oz self-raising flour sifted on to paper

For the filling

1 tin (19 oz, 550 grams) marrons au sirop

8 oz cream cheese

1 tsp icing sugar

1 tsp vanilla essence

6 fl oz double cream

For the decoration

Extra icing sugar

Double cream

Vanilla essence

Butter a tin 14 × 9 inches with unsalted butter, then line its base with greaseproof paper also buttered. Whisk the eggs, sugar and essence until thick and the whisk leaves a very distinct trail. Briskly whisk in the flour and incorporate the melted, cool butter at the same time. Pour into the lined tin. Spread the mixture particularly into the corners. Bake at gas mark 5, 375°F (190°C) for 12 minutes.

Make the filling: roughly chop the marrons, having drained them (reserve 4 or 5 for decoration if you like). Beat the cheese with the icing sugar and vanilla. Whip the cream until it stands in soft peaks, and carefully fold into the cream cheese (don't try to combine these stages in a machine or you will most likely end up with a curdled mess).

Have ready a damp, clean tea-towel, well wrung out in cold water. Invert the sponge on this, remove the base paper. Leave to cool but not get cold, or it won't roll successfully. Spread liberally with the mixture, and roll up gently but firmly using the towel to hold all together as you roll.

Leave to cool completely. Dredge liberally with icing sugar and decorate at will with extra whipped cream and marrons. (The cream should be whipped with half a teaspoon of icing sugar and a drop or two of vanilla.)

Chocolate cake

Serves 8

8 oz butter	Pinch salt
8 oz castor sugar	7 oz dark chocolate
4 eggs	4 fl oz double cream
6 oz self-raising flour	1 dsp redcurrant jelly
2 oz cocoa powder	Water or sherry

Well butter two 7 inch sandwich tins. Sift together flour, cocoa and salt. Cream butter and sugar thoroughly. Whip the eggs and gradually beat these into the creamed mixture adding a spoonful of flour as you go along. Lightly mix in the balance of the flour mixture. Add a little water (or sherry) to achieve a soft dropping consistency. Spoon the mixture into the two tins and bake at gas mark 4, 350°F (180°C) for 40 to 45 minutes. Turn onto a wire cooling tray.

Put the chocolate and jelly into a basin over boiling water; stir until melted and smooth. Beat in the cream; leave to cool; spread over the cake and between the two layers.

Extra interest can be added to this cake if a layer of redcurrant jelly is spread on the bottom cake before spreading the chocolate cream filling.

Othello layer cake

Serves 8 to 10

This dark-faced cake is a speciality in Denmark, where it is baked for birthdays and celebrations.

The cake base
3 whole eggs
1 tsp vanilla essence
(I prefer to keep a vanilla pod
   in my sugar jar)

4 oz castor sugar
3 oz self-raising flour

The cream filling
1 oz castor sugar
1 level tsp plain flour
2 egg yolks

$\frac{1}{3}$ pint double cream
3 tbsp whipped cream
Castor sugar

The jam filling
4 oz apricot jam, sieved

Chocolate icing
4 oz plain chocolate (use only
   the best quality)
4 oz castor sugar dissolved in 2
   tbsp water

1 tsp flavourless oil or liquid
   paraffin, or glycerine
$\frac{1}{2}$ pint whipping cream

Line three baking sheets with buttered greaseproof paper. With a pencil, inscribe a circle on each, using an 8 inch flan ring as a template.

Beat the eggs together with the vanilla and sugar until white and thick. If you can see a trail left by the beater when it is drawn slowly through the mixture, then it is thick enough. Fold in the sifted flour with a slotted spoon. Spoon equally on to three sheets and spread with a palette knife to the shape of the circles.

Bake these thin 'pancakes' in a preheated oven at gas mark 6, 400°F (200°C) for 10–12 minutes. Turn on to a cooling rack and remove the papers. Allow to cool and, again using the flan ring as a template, trim the layers to shape.

Make the cream filling: cream the sugar, flour and yolks together, add the double cream which has been heated to boiling point, then put all in a double boiler or stand the basin over a pan of boiling water. Allow the sauce to cook for a minute, stirring continuously. Cool, sprinkling the surface with a little castor sugar to avoid a skin forming. When cold, incorporate a further 3 tablespoons of whipped cream, lightly sweetened, to lighten the filling somewhat.

For the jam filling: put the apricot jam into a basin over hot water until it becomes soft. Press this through a wire sieve and allow to cool. Spread the jam on to one base, covering this with a second cake on to which you can then spread your cream filling, topping it with the third base.

Now make the chocolate icing. Melt the chocolate in a basin over hot water. Mix in the glycerine. Boil the sugar syrup to 'small thread' on a sugar thermometer. If you don't possess one, boil the syrup until it looks thick. *Do not stir, or the sugar will crystallise.*

Allow the sugar syrup to cool a little, then pour into the melted chocolate, beating until a coating consistency is achieved. If you end up with a solid-looking fudge in your pan, don't panic – all is not lost. Restore the consistency by adding hot water a tablespoon at a time, beating well.

You will have to work fairly quickly with this icing. A palette knife and a jug of boiling water into which you can frequently dip it will facilitate this operation. Spread it over the top and decorate the sides with the whipped cream.

Fruit

Baked stuffed peaches

Serves 4

Allow one whole or two half peaches per head. This dish is at its best when made with fresh peaches, but canned ones are a reasonable substitute.

4 peaches
2 oz castor sugar
Finely grated rind of one
    lemon
2 tbsp cocoa
4 oz sweet almonds, chopped

5–6 ginger biscuits, crumbled
    finely (or amaretto biscuits)
1 tbsp brandy
1 egg
2 oz unsalted butter
Extra sugar for dredging

Bring a pan of water to the boil. Plunge the peaches in for a minute. Remove with a slotted spoon into a bowl of cold water. When cool enough to handle, skin them, cut them in half and remove the stone. Scoop out some of the peach pulp to enlarge the cavity somewhat. Put this into a bowl. Arrange the peach halves in a fireproof dish.

Mix the remaining ingredients, apart from the butter, together in a bowl to form a stiff paste. Divide this paste equally between the eight peach halves: dot with butter and sprinkle with a little castor sugar.

Bake in a pre-heated oven at gas mark 5, 375°F (190°C) for about half an hour or until the peaches are tender but not collapsing.

Serve with cream or, for an extra treat, Zabaglione.

Strawberry bliss

Serves 4

1 lb strawberries, hulled and
    cut into quarters
4 level tbsp castor sugar
2 tbsp Crême de Caçao (or
    one miniature bottle)

2 tbsp Cointreau or Grand
    Marnier
1 tsp finely grated orange rind

About an hour before dinner time, toss all the ingredients together: cover with plastic film and chill.

Serve quite simply: just like that!

An added extra would be to sprinkle with a little grated dark chocolate.

An even better added extra would be to add the grated chocolate and then mask the fruits with whipped cream lightly sweetened.

Pears in lemon juice

Serves 6

6 pears
2 lemons
1 tsp vanilla essence

¾ pint water
1 lb castor sugar

With a potato peeler remove the zest (yellow part) of the lemons. Shred this with a sharp knife as finely as possible. Dissolve the sugar in the water together with the vanilla and lemon rind; simmer until the syrup is quite clear. Peel the pears from bottom to tip, leaving them whole and leaving the stalk intact. Rub well with lemon juice to keep their good colour.

Select a pan into which the pears just fit when tightly packed; squeeze the lemon juice, add to the syrup and pour this over the pears. If it doesn't quite cover them, fix a piece of foil over the tips of each pear (this is only to prevent discolouration). Simmer the pears until just tender. Remove them to a dish and whilst they are cooling, reduce the syrup to half its former quantity. Let this cool, pour over the pears and chill well. Serve with plenty of unsweetened whipped cream, or lemon sorbet.

Those who saw *The Duchess of Duke Street* episode where Louisa Trotter makes this delicate dish will have noticed that the lemon rind appears in long candied strips. This is achieved by the use of a 'cannelle' knife obtainable from any good kitchen shop. The syrup is then, in the last stages, reduced until thick and viscous and the lemon peel totally candied and edible.

Wardens in red wine

Serves 8

Wardens being pears: the recipe comes from a book by a Doncaster cook in 1740, not from the stoves of France as you might imagine. You can use either eating or cooking pears.

½ pint Burgundy type red wine
3 oz Demerara sugar
1 orange

6 cloves
8 good pears
A little red colouring

Remove orange rind with a potato peeler and shred as fine as hairs. Squeeze the juice. Put wine, sugar, rind, juice and cloves into a pan. Simmer for 5 minutes.

Peel, core and quarter the pears. Cover with the hot wine syrup and poach until just tender. Leave to cool, then chill well. Serve with ice cream or whipped sour cream for a change.

Baked spicy dates
Serves 6

1 dozen large fresh pitted dates
3 egg yolks

1 tbsp rum or brandy
½ pint double cream

For the filling
2 oz ground almonds
1 oz pistachio nuts, roughly crushed
1 oz candied orange peel, chopped
1 oz seedless raisins (muscatels), chopped

1 oz walnuts, roughly chopped
1 oz stem ginger, chopped or shredded
1 tbsp good honey
1 level tsp ground ginger
1 level tsp ground cinnamon

Combine all the filling ingredients into a soft paste. Pack each date with plenty of this mixture.

Take 6 small ramekins or cocottes and place 2 stuffed dates in each. Combine yolks, rum and cream (no sugar unless you like things very sweet) and pour this mixture around the filled dates. Stand the little dishes in a bain-marie and bake at gas mark 4, 350°F (180°C) for 20–30 minutes or until the custard is set.

Serve hot or warm.

Victorian prune jelly
Serves 6

12 oz giant prunes
½ pint red wine
2 oz castor sugar
¼ pint orange juice
1 level tsp cinnamon

1 level tsp grated orange rind
1 tsp vanilla essence
½ oz gelatine crystals *see* Method
Extra orange juice

Bring to the boil the wine, sugar and orange juice. Add the cinnamon, orange rind and vanilla essence, then the prunes.

Poach gently until tender. Drain the prunes, and if necessary make the liquid up to ¾ pint with more orange juice. Bring this to the boil, remove the pan from the heat, stir in the gelatine (if the weather is warm use ¾ oz gelatine). Leave to cool somewhat whilst you pit the prunes.

Put the prune flesh and the wine syrup into a blender and blend until smooth. Pour into a wetted mould and put to set.

Turn out and decorate with whipped cream and extra prunes and some toasted flaked almonds if you are feeling in a lavish mood.

It is an excellent notion to poach extra prunes for a garnish in a light caramel syrup, removing them when cooked and reducing the syrup until viscous and sticky.

Pruneaux au Bourgogne (Prunes soaked in Burgundy)

Serves 4 or 5

This unusual though simple way of preparing prunes is delicious and effective if served with dollops of chilled unsweetened whipped cream.

1 lb giant prunes	6 oz vanilla sugar
1 pint hot water	1 bottle red Burgundy

Soak the prunes overnight in 1 pint of hot water. Having soaked the prunes, drain them and further pat them dry. Make the vanilla sugar by leaving a vanilla pod in the sugar jar for a week.

Place the prunes in a dish, scatter with the sugar and pour over the Burgundy.

Leave them to soak for a further 24 hours (no cooking) before chilling.

Rum-blazed bananas with almonds and chocolate

Serves 4

4 bananas, skinned, halved lengthways, then quartered	½ tsp grated orange rind
	Juice of an orange
Juice of half a lemon	2 fl oz Jamaican or Demerara
1½ oz unsalted butter	rum
1½ oz castor sugar	

Decoration

1 oz toasted almonds

2 oz coarsely grated chocolate
  (or a crumbled flake)

¼ pint cream for pouring

Bathe the bananas in the lemon juice to keep them white. Cover with plastic film until ready for cooking.

Melt the butter with the sugar in a shallow pan, preferably an enamel one, add the orange rind and juice and simmer until it has a syrupy consistency.

Add the bananas. Baste them over a low heat for two to three minutes until they are just cooked.

Warm the rum in a large metal soup ladle over a low heat. Pour over the bananas, tip the pan to the flame or ignite with a match. Sprinkle over the chocolate whilst still flaming, scatter the almonds over and serve with pouring cream.

Rhubarb compôte

Serves 4

I prefer to call it stewed rhubarb, for that is what it is, but there are those who find this title off-putting and reminiscent of schooldays when rhubarb appeared like Emu knitting wool afloat in two quarts of acetic acid!

1 lb rhubarb *see* Method

2 oz stem ginger

6 oz brown sugar, or more

1 level tsp powdered ginger

1 large lemon

Select rhubarb stalks of even thickness – a small point you might well think, but so important when it comes to cooking things evenly – cut into pieces of equal length approximately 1½ inches long. Take a baking dish large enough to contain your pieces in *one* layer. Chop or slice the ginger and distribute between the pieces of rhubarb.

Mix the ground ginger and sugar, then sprinkle evenly over the fruit. With a potato-peeler remove the rind of at least half the lemon. (If your patience is non-existent, *grate* the rind; otherwise make a chiffonade (the rind, cut into hair-fine strips) but don't be too heavy handed, for you mustn't take any of the white pith off, as this is the bitter part.)

Squeeze the nude lemon and pour the juice, with the rind,

over the contents of your dish. Cover with a lid or foil and bake gently in the oven until the fruit is *just* tender. Chill well.

Attention to detail and acceptance of a bit of fuss will produce the right effect. If you cut down on the sugar content and hack up your rhubarb any old how, then you can expect wet string!

Exotic fruit salad with Turkish delight

Serves 6

This combination is very exciting and you will get a good deal of praise from those who enjoy rich dishes: yet there is little or no work to do and nothing to go wrong!

1 medium-sized pineapple	6 oz almond Turkish delight
4 kiwi fruits	Whipped cream (optional)
Juice of half a lemon	Chocolate sauce (see page 137)

Halve the pineapple top to bottom, leaving the foliage on each half. Using a grapefruit knife, carefully scoop out the pineapple flesh, cut away any tough core, chop the pineapple into bite-size pieces, and return the fruit to the shell halves.

Peel the kiwi fruits with a potato peeler, and cut into discs. Splash with the lemon juice and leave to soak for half an hour.

Arrange the kiwi fruits around the pineapple halves and fill the centre with small pieces of Turkish delight. You can pipe a band of cream down the centre. The sauce can be served hot or cold.

Melon salad with Pernod and mint

Serves 4

1 ripe honeydew melon	2 fl oz Pernod or Ricard
Up to 2 oz of castor sugar	5 or 6 mint leaves

Cut the melon in half. Take out the seeds and discard them. With the small bowl of a melon baller (or Parisienne spoon) scoop out the flesh into a bowl.

Sprinkle with castor sugar, toss well. Add the Pernod or Ricard and the mint leaves. Chill well covered with plastic film.

Serve with a sugared mint leaf as decoration – coat both sides of a mint leaf with egg white, dip in castor sugar, and chill.

Nectarines baked in cream

Serves 6

Simple sweets are invariably effective. Here is a nectarine sweet to add to your collection.

6 nectarines	2 × 6 oz cartons double cream
6 rounded tbsp castor sugar	1 vanilla pod

Skin, pit and quarter the nectarines. Place them rather close together in a shallow baking dish.

Sprinkle the castor sugar over the fruit, and pour the cream over them. Lay a vanilla pod among the fruit, and place in the oven at gas mark 4, 350°F (180°C) for 30 minutes or until they are tender. (Vanilla pods are obtainable at health food shops, and are an essential part of this dish. They can be washed under the cold tap and used again.)

Serve ice cold.

One variation on this theme is to make a pie by adding a sweet pastry crust. Yet another is to serve the nectarines with balls of chocolate ice-cream. This recipe works equally well with fresh dessert pears or large dessert plums.

Strawberries cardinal

Serves 6 or 8

This classical dish is so easy to make and so very rewarding to eat. Its success lies in the quality of the strawberries and raspberries and the one simple technique of cutting the strawberries in half so that the cut face absorbs the delicious raspberry purée.

Having created such an elegant dish – and simplicity *is* elegance – I think it almost criminal to blanket the fruits with cream – but, of course, the choice is yours.

2 lb strawberries	2 oz castor sugar (or less)
¾ lb raspberries	2 tbsp lemon juice

Pick over the strawberries. Unless they are very sandy, do not wash them. With a stainless-steel knife cut them in half (carbon steel will taint the fruit). If they are huge, quarter them.

Pick over the raspberries. Put into a stainless-steel or enamel-lined pan with the lemon juice and sugar. Over a minimal heat soften the fruit, letting it gradually come to the boil. Stir from time to time. Simmer for 1–2 minutes (longer will remove the 'fresh' flavour of the raspberries). Cool.

Rub through a fine-meshed sieve. (Do not blend or you will end up with a cloudy purée and will still have all the seeds to get rid of!) Cool, then chill.

An hour before serving, gently turn the cut strawberries into the purée, using a large slotted spoon and a large bowl.

Pile them into polished glass dishes or one large glass bowl. This is one of the few occasions when glass – and cut-glass in particular – complements food.

Queen Alexandra's summer pudding

Serves 4

4 oz fresh white breadcrumbs   2 oz castor sugar
2 oz unsalted butter

Purée
1 lb apples   3 oz sugar or to taste
2 oz unsalted butter   2 tsp vanilla essence

Topping
⅓ pint whipping cream   Flaked sweet almonds
                                        (optional)

Melt the butter in a frying pan. Toss the sugar and crumbs together, then over a very low heat fry these until crisp and golden brown. This will take some time and will need constant turning and moving about of the crumbs in the pan to ensure even colouring and a good nutty flavour. Leave to cool completely.

Peel and core apples, slice thinly and evenly. Melt the butter in a pan, add apples, sugar and essence. Simmer over a low heat. Purée on a blender, put to cool.

Arrange crumbs in layers in a glass bowl with the purée (or other stewed fruits). Top with a thick layer of whipped cream and flaked almonds.

Orange salad

Serves 4

This is the simplest and most effective of sweets to serve after a rich main course.

4 oranges
Castor sugar

Orange flower water

With a sharp knife peel the oranges, segment them, dredge with castor sugar and a good splash of orange flower water, and put to chill.

Danish apple and raspberry pudding

Serves 6

This was my favourite pudding back in the days when I was living as a young man in Copenhagen. It is in every Danish housewife's repertory, each woman giving her special slant to things. I make mine with a fresh raspberry purée in place of the more usual raspberry jam.

4 oz unsalted butter
1 oz castor sugar
2 breakfast cups of coarse
    white breadcrumbs
    see Method
1 pint apple purée made from
    2 lb Cox's apples

Raspberry purée (see below)
½ to ¾ pint double cream
    whipped to soft peak, lightly
    sweetened
Toasted almonds for garnish
    (optional luxury)

The most effective way to make this pudding is to hand-pluck the breadcrumbs: this gives more texture to things. If you can't be bothered to do this then use the coarse side of a grater, or make them carefully in a blender, taking them out whilst they are still coarse.

Melt the butter evenly in a large skillet or frying pan, swirling it round so that it doesn't burn. Mix the crumbs and sugar well together. Turn these into the foaming butter, lower the heat to almost minimum and let the crumbs acquire a good colour and get crisp right through. You will have to stir and turn them all the time to ensure that the full nutty flavour is obtained. Spread thinly on a large flat plate, and leave them to cool.

Choose a nice serving bowl and put in a layer of crumbs, then a layer of apple purée, a second layer of crumbs which is then topped with a layer of raspberry purée, and finally decorate with a thick cushion of whipped cream sprinkled with the toasted almonds.

Raspberry purée
8 oz frozen raspberries, defrosted
1 oz castor sugar

Juice of 1 large lemon (use the rind in the apple purée)

Put all the ingredients into a pan and stir over a low heat until a soft purée is arrived at (about 5 minutes). Leave to cool.

Ice-cream sweets

'Smith on a sundae'

Serves 4

6 oz raspberries (fresh or frozen in dry sugar)
8 oz block vanilla ice-cream
4 oz crushed almond praline (see instructions below)

6 fl oz chocolate sauce (see below)
½ pint whipped unsweetened cream
A few whole almonds for garnish

The chocolate sauce
6 oz plain block chocolate
4 oz castor sugar
2 tsp cocoa

1 pint water
A few drops of vanilla essence.

Break up the chocolate and place it in a heavy-bottomed pan with the other ingredients for the chocolate sauce. Heat gently until the chocolate and the sugar are dissolved: then simmer for 30 minutes or until the sauce looks rich and syrupy. Make this the day before so that it gets really cold.

To make the almond praline: put 2 oz castor sugar in to a small pan. Heat *gently* until it becomes a caramel (do not stir or add any water), then add 2 oz flaked almonds and remove from the heat.

Mix the almonds into the caramel and tip out on to an oiled piece of foil. When cold, crush with your rolling pin or in your blender. This can be stored in a screw-top jar for many weeks.

To make the sundae, have all the ingredients and four tall glasses ready in your refrigerator. Have your whipped cream in a piping bag for easy handling, then all you have to do is quickly fill your glasses with alternate layers of ice-cream, praline, fruit, chocolate sauce – finishing the filled glasses with a swirl of cream and popping the whole almonds on as a garnish.

Original peach Melba

Created by The Savoy Hotel's great chef Auguste Escoffier in honour of the glass-shattering soprano, Dame Nellie Melba. This sweet can be built up at will and is at its best when served in the grand style of the Edwardian era and not in individual glasses; this also makes matters easier for today's hostess.

Vanilla ice-cream
Fresh peaches (allow one
    whole peach per head)
Lemon juice

Whipped cream
Sugar
Vanilla essence
Flaked almonds

Sauce
8 oz frozen raspberries
Juice of one lemon

3 oz castor sugar
2 tbsp gin, kirsch or cold water

Make the sauce by simmering all the ingredients together for 5 minutes. Whilst it is not essential to strain the sauce it is finer if you do so through a coarse sieve. Allow to cool then chill well.

Skin the peaches by plunging them into boiling water for a few seconds; cut them in half, remove the stone and rub the flesh well with lemon juice to prevent discolouration. Arrange balls of vanilla ice-cream in a large shallow glass dish, press a peach cap on top of each ball, coat with chilled raspberry sauce, decorate liberally with vanilla flavoured sweetened whipped cream and flaked almonds.

Almond and apricot vacherin

Serves 6 to 8

Cake bases
5 egg whites
10 oz castor sugar

6 oz toasted, crushed almonds

Custard ice-cream
8 egg yolks
1 pint single cream (or half
   cream, half milk)

3 oz castor sugar
1 tsp almond extract

Filling
Apricot halves
Whipped cream

Liqueur (optional)
Icing sugar

To make the cake bases, stiffly beat the egg whites as for meringues, incorporating half the sugar as you beat and the second half towards the end of the beating when the meringue mixture must stand up in peaks.

Using a slotted spoon, fold in the crushed almonds. Divide the mixture between two 8 inch sandwich tins lined with silicone paper. Bake at gas mark 5, 375°F (190°C) for 35–40 minutes. Leave to cool a little before turning on to a wire cooling tray and removing the papers.

The meringue bases can be made days in advance and stored in an airtight container tin or even frozen.

Next, make the custard ice-cream. Beat the egg yolks and sugar until fluffy and all the granules are dissolved. Bring the cream and almond extract to the boil, and pour over the egg mixture, whisking briskly all the time. Arrange the bowl over a pan of boiling water and, stirring gently all the time, thicken the custard until it is the consistency of good cream and well coats the back of a wooden spoon (if you draw your fingers across the back of the spoon it should leave a definite trail).

Leave the custard to cool completely: then chill it either following the instructions on your ice-cream machine or in a suitable container which will fit into the ice-making compartment of your refrigerator or deep freeze, in which case stir the mixture every half-hour to prevent ice crystals from forming.

To form the ice-cream layer: line one of the sandwich tins used for the meringue bases with plastic film. Press the ice-cream into this to make a thick 'cake'. Chill until ready for use.

To assemble the vacherin: invert one of the meringue cake bases on to a platter. Unmould the ice-cream removing the plastic film on top of this. Pipe a collar of whipped cream round the edge of the ice-cream. Fill with the apricot halves, splash with a suitable liqueur such as Amaretto, Crème de Banane, or Kirsch.

Rest the second meringue on top of all this. Dredge liberally with icing sugar.

Prince of Wales pudding
Serves 6 or 8

This pudding can only be assembled just before serving, but everything can be at the ready: top caramelised; ice-cream in the refrigerator; raspberries already in the bottom layer on a serving dish; sauce keeping warm over hot, but not boiling, water; sauce boat and ladle ready to receive this.

1 large sponge cake   Raspberries
Chocolate ice-cream

Topping
3 oz castor sugar   3 tbsp water

Sauce
7 oz dark chocolate   1 tsp vanilla essence
6 tbsp cold water   1 egg yolk
1 oz unsalted butter

First make the topping. Put the castor sugar together with the water into a pan. Let this slowly caramelise. Split the cake in half. Stand the cake top on a cake tray over a large plate (or piece of foil). Gently pour the boiling caramel over the top and leave to cool and harden.

To make hot chocolate sauce, arrange a basin over a pan of boiling water. Break chocolate into pieces and put into the basin with all the other ingredients (except the egg yolk). When all is dissolved and hot, remove the basin from the heat and quickly whisk in the egg yolk. Stand the basin over warm (not boiling) water until ready for serving. Serve the hot sauce separately.

Scoop out some of the crumbs from the bottom cake half, fill with fresh or frozen raspberries. Pile in scoops of chocolate ice-cream. Balance the caramelised lid on top.

Pancakes

Brandied apple pancakes

Serves 6

The batter

4 oz soft plain white flour,
   sieved
1 oz castor sugar
2 whole eggs
4 egg yolks

½ pint milk or more
Grated zest of a small lemon
   (about a tsp)
3 oz unsalted butter, melted
   but cool

The apple filling

2 lb Cox's or Starking apples
Juice of 1 lemon
Juice of 1 orange

Strips of rind off both
1 oz unsalted butter
2 oz castor sugar, or to taste

½ lb apricot jam, sieved

The topping

Icing sugar
3 fl oz brandy or Calvados

½ pint thick pouring cream

To make the batter: sieve the flour and sugar together with the lemon zest in to a mixing bowl. Beat the whole eggs and the egg yolks together with half a pint of the milk. Make a well in the flour mixture and pour this in. Gradually incorporate the flour and beat well. Strain into a clean bowl to rid the mixture of any possible lumps. Incorporate more milk if necessary until you have a batter the consistency of thin cream. Stir in the melted butter: you will not need to grease your pan if you follow this method – you will also get 'lacier' pancakes.

Make up wafer-thin pancakes using a spanking hot heavy-bottomed frying-pan about 7 inches in diameter. This quantity of batter will make at least 20 pancakes.

To make the apple filling: peel, core and slice the apples. Simmer over a low heat in a lidded pan together with the orange and lemon juice. Remove the strips of fruit rind. Mash the apples to a pulp. It should be soft but not too wet: if it is, then let the pulp bubble over a low heat until it has dried out somewhat.

To make up the pancakes: clear your worktop and lay out all the pancakes. Spread sieved apricot jam on one quarter of each pancake, and apple purée on the adjacent quarter. Fold the clean half of the pancake over, then fold carefully into quarters.

Arrange them in a shallow buttered flameproof dish slightly overlapping (everything up to this point can be done in advance).

Serving and blazing the pancakes: Pre-heat the oven to gas mark 5, 375°F (190°C). Pre-heat the grill. Warm the pancakes through in the oven for 15 minutes. Using a fine wire sieve dredge the top of the pancakes with a goodly coating of icing sugar. Wipe the edges of the dish and slide it under the hot grill to caramelise the sugar.

Stand the hot dish on a serving platter. Warm the brandy in a small pan, pour over the pancakes and ignite at the table. Baste them well with the liquor. Serve with pouring cream – allow three per serving.

Crêpes au Kirsch (Apricot pancakes flamed with Kirsch)

Serves 4 or 5

Batter for 12 to 14 pancakes
8 oz sifted plain white flour
2 oz castor sugar
3 whole eggs
1 egg yolk

1 level tsp grated lemon rind
   or tsp vanilla essence
Up to 1 pint milk
2 egg whites
Pinch of salt

Melted butter for frying

Filling
Sieved apricot jam or purée of
   apricots
Castor sugar

Kirsch or light rum, Akvavit,
   Framboise

Sift flour, sugar and salt into a bowl. Beat the whole eggs and yolk together and gradually incorporate into the flour, adding the rind or vanilla essence at the same time. Add enough of the milk to make a very free-flowing batter. Leave to rest and chill in the refrigerator for an hour or two.

Just before making the pancakes, fold in the stiffly-beaten egg whites.

Using a spanking hot pan, brush the base lightly with butter, hold the pan at 45°, float over a film of the batter, twisting the pan to ensure an even, thin covering. Fry quickly on both sides.

Turn the pancake onto an inverted soup plate. (This is simply to make it easier to pick them up again.)

Spread each all over with a good layer of the fruit purée. Fold in half and in half again.

Arrange, overlapping slightly, in a lightly-buttered ovenproof dish. Sprinkle with castor sugar.

Cover with foil and keep them warm in the oven at the lowest temperature.

Just before serving, gently warm the Kirsch in a small pan (allow one tablespoon per two pancakes). Pour over the pancakes and ignite.

Pancakes stuffed with raisins, walnuts and chocolate
Serves 5 to 6

Pancake Batter

4 oz soft plain white flour, sieved
1 oz castor sugar
2 whole eggs
4 egg yolks

Up to ½ pint milk
Grated zest of a small lemon (about a teaspoon)
3 oz unsalted butter, melted but cool

Filling

4 oz unsalted butter
2 oz castor sugar
1 tbsp rum
4 oz walnuts, crushed

2 oz muscatel seedless raisins, chopped
4 oz grated chocolate (or chocolate flake)

Make pancake batter as for Brandied apple pancakes (page 196). Reserve, and prepare filling. Cream the butter and sugar until light and fluffy. Beat in the rum. Mix in the walnuts and chopped muscatels.

As each pancake is made, slide on to an upturned soup plate arranged over a pan of simmering water. Cover with a clean cloth to keep warm.

When ready to serve, spread with the butter mixture, roll or fold. Arrange in a serving dish, sprinkle with grated chocolate, and serve before the chocolate melts entirely.

Quire of paper

Serves 6

Batter

4 oz plain flour
2 eggs plus 2 extra yolks
¼ pint milk
¼ pint single cream

4 tbsp sherry, brandy or water
1 oz castor sugar
Butter for frying

Filling

2 oz unsalted butter
2 oz icing sugar
Juice ½ lemon

½ tsp grated lemon rind
Raspberry purée or raspberry
   jam

Beat together eggs, yolks, cream, sugar and milk. Sieve the flour into a bowl and make a well. Pour in the liquid and gradually incorporate the flour until you have a smooth batter. Add the sherry, brandy or water until your batter is the consistency of cream.

Rub a frying pan with buttered paper or 1 teaspoon clarified butter. Fry the pancakes as thin as possible.

Cream together the butter, icing sugar and lemon juice and rind to make a lemon butter cream. Spread pancakes alternatively with lemon butter cream and fresh raspberry purée or a good raspberry jam. To make a quire stack them in piles of 20 (actually 10 is enough).

To serve, cut in wedges like a cake.

Breads and tea cakes

Nellie Smith's Harvo bread

2 teacups brown flour
2 teacups white flour
1 teacup sultanas, dates or
   raisins
½ teacup sugar

1 teacup golden syrup
Approx ½ teacup milk
1 tsp bicarbonate of soda
2 oz lard

Melt the syrup and lard together and stir in the bicarbonate of soda. Add to dry ingredients and mix well. Add enough milk to make a dropping consistency. Bake in 1 lb loaf tins (well buttered) at gas mark 4, 350°F (180°C), for about an hour or until a knife inserted into the middle comes out clean.

Freda Lord's date and walnut loaf

12 oz self-raising flour
8 oz sugar
3 oz margarine
1 large egg
1 tsp salt

6 oz dates
4 oz walnuts
1 tsp bicarbonate of soda
⅓ pint boiling water

Mix the bicarbonate of soda into the boiling water and pour over the roughly-chopped dates and leave to soak.

Sift the flour and rub in the margarine. Add the sugar, chopped walnuts and salt. Mash the dates well into the water and soda mixture, and add with the beaten egg to the dry ingredients. Mix well. Bake at gas mark 2, 300°F (150°C), in a 2 lb-size loaf tin (well buttered) for 1½ hours.

Rye bread

2½ lb rye flour (medium
   milled)
1 heaped tsp salt
1 tsp sugar
4 oz lard, melted but not hot

1 pint warm milk (sour milk is
   good for this bread)
½ oz fresh or ¼ oz dried yeast

Put flour and salt in a mixing bowl. Cream the yeast in a little of the milk with the sugar. Make a well and pour in the melted lard and blood-warm milk and yeast mixture. Work into a mass and then knead for 15 minutes, or until the dough is springy, smooth and 'shiny'.

Leave this to rise, covered with a damp cloth or in a large polythene bag, for 1½–2 hours. Cut into 2 large or 4 small shapes, to half-fill buttered bread tins. Knead lightly and place in tins.

Leave to prove for 45 minutes, when they should be soft and spongy. Bake at gas mark 7–8, 425°–450°F (220°–230°C) for 30 minutes, then lower the temperature 1 degree for a further 20 minutes.

Savoury herb bread

8 oz self-raising flour
1 heaped tsp salt
1 level tsp dry mustard
1 tbsp mixed herbs (or 1 tsp
  dried thyme and sage,
1 tbsp freshly chopped parsley)
3 oz 'dry' Cheddar cheese,
  grated
1 egg, beaten
1½ oz butter

Mix all dry ingredients together, including the cheese. Melt the butter and add to the dry ingredients together with the beaten egg. Stir until well mixed. Place in a buttered 1 lb loaf tin and bake at gas mark 5, 375°F (190°C), for 35–40 minutes. Cool before removing from tin.

Banana nut loaf

2 oz unsalted butter
2 oz castor sugar
6 fl oz honey (half a 12 oz jar)
2 large eggs
3 ripe bananas
9 oz plain flour (or wholemeal)
3 level tsp baking powder
2 oz chopped nuts (almonds,
  walnuts or hazelnuts)

This recipe can be made with a blender or as follows:

Cream butter and sugar. Beat in honey. Add eggs and beat well. Well mash the bananas and mix in. Sift together flour and baking powder, and fold into mixture. Finally fold in the nuts.

Bake in a buttered loaf tin (2 lb size) for ¾ hour at gas mark 5, 375°F (190°C), and then reduce to gas mark 4, 350°F (180°C) and bake for a further ½ hour, or until risen and firm to the touch.

If almonds or hazelnuts are used, toast these lightly for a different flavour.

Sally Lunn

This is an 18th-century recipe.

9 oz plain flour
¼ tsp salt
½ oz fresh yeast or 2 tsp dried
    yeast

1 egg
1 oz white sugar
¼ pint thick cream

Sift the flour and salt into a warmed bowl. Make a well in the centre.

Put the fresh yeast in a separate bowl and cream with 4 tablespoons lukewarm water. If using dried yeast, dissolve it in 4 tablespoons hand-hot water, and leave for 10 minutes to froth. Whisk the egg and sugar together in a separate bowl and pour this, the yeast, and thick cream into the well in the centre of the flour. Mix to a dough, then cover with a damp, folded cloth, and leave for 1½ hours to rise in a warm place.

Punch the dough down then beat by hand until the dough is shiny and starts leaving the side of the bowl and your hand clean. This will take about 8–10 minutes, hard work. Spoon the mixture into a greased, lined 6 inch cake tin. Cover again with the damp cloth, and leave until the dough has risen to the top of the tin. Bake on the shelf just below the centre of the oven at gas mark 7, 425°F (220°C), for 30 minutes. After 15 minutes, place a sheet of paper over the top of the tea cake to protect it from over browning.

When baked, remove from the tin and strip off the papers. Leave to cool a little on a wire rack. When warm slice three equal rounds and spread with softened, salty butter. Transfer to the warm oven to melt the butter, then serve immediately, cut in wedges.

Index